PHILIPPIANS

Where Life Advances

Roy L. Laurin

KREGEL PUBLICATIONS
Grand Rapids, Michigan 49501

Philippians: Where Life Advances by Roy L. Laurin.
Published 1987 by Kregel Publications, a division
of Kregel, Inc. All rights reserved.

Library of Congress Cataloging-in-Publication Data

Laurin, Roy L. (Roy Leonard), 1898-1966.
  Philippians: Where Life Advances.

  Reprint. Originally published: Findlay, Ohio: Dunham
Pub. Co., 1955.
  1. Bible. N.T. Philippians—Commentaries.
I. Title.
BS2704.3.L38   1986   227'.606   86-7177
ISBN 0-8254-3134-4
2 3 4 5 6 Printing/Year 91 90 89 88 87

CONTENTS

PREFACE

The original material of this and other volumes of the "Life" series was developed and prepared for radio presentation. Its style came out of that particular purpose and it is hoped that it will be found equally profitable for reading and study.

Books are like sermons as sermons are like recipes, the work of a life time. Sermons are words but they are more. They are living things. They are people, experiences, death beds and funerals. They are understandings that comes out of the perfidy of a friend, the slander of an enemy, the agony of personal moral struggles, the prayers of the study and struggles of life.

The author is indebted to much help from others, some of which is without identification but wherever possible the source is indicated.

Roy L. Laurin

INTRODUCTION

In Paul's Epistle to the Philippians we look at Christian life in terms of experience. As experience the Christian life is not static or sterile: it is constantly advancing, climbing, achieving and reproducing. Here is to be found the secret and scope of the Christian life in terms of its advancement and enlargement.

There is an essential distinction which we must make between Christianity as doctrine and Christianity as experience. As doctrine Christianity never changes. As experience Christianity is always changing. Language in terms of the alphabet never changes for these twenty-six building blocks of language are always the same. But language as the expression of thought is always changing. Semanticists are constantly finding new word meanings. We are constantly using new word combinations. In chemistry the elements are changeless while the compounds are limitless and never static. In music the basic notes and chords are beyond change, whereas the combinations of notes and chords are in constant conception of change.

When one reads Philippians he will be aware of the changeless nature of its doctrines of God, of Christ, of revelation and of salvation while observing the ever-advancing and changing nature of the experiences based upon these doctrines. Men are saved in the same unchanging manner in our century that they were in Paul's century. But the experience of this salvation is not limited to certain predetermined boundaries of thought and emotion. It goes on as Paul expresses it in this epistle as a "reaching forth unto those things which are before" (Phil. 3:13). This means life advancing.

The changeless source and center of this advancing life is Jesus Christ. It is this: "For to me to live is Christ . . ." (Phil. 1:21). This is the essence of Christianity. This is its highest truth. If this is Bible truth in a nutshell, it is also Christian experience in a life-full, for here is fullness of experience and blessing.

"Christian experience is not something which is going on around the believer, but something which is going on in him. . . . Right Christian experience is the outworking, whatever one's circumstances may be, of the life, nature and mind of Christ living in us" (C. I. Scofield). This means that Christian experience is not the achievement of a human effort but a divine effect. Jesus never told men to try to live as He lived by imitation but to let Him live in them by divine initiative.

This epistle does not censure the Philippian church for errors in doctrine, nor blame it for irregularities of life. It does anticipate the dangers of error and the possibility of irregularity but it deals rather, as Arthur S. Way says, with the peril of over-independence and perhaps self-sufficiency. "In no other epistle so much as in this has Paul multiplied the expressions of love and praise of his readers: a strong testimony certainly as to the praiseworthy condition of the church" (Meyer's Commentary).

Tacitly it is a warning against the danger of a static spirituality and a stationary Christian experience. It is likewise a challenge to an advancing, progressing life of Christian fullness and effectiveness.

By a static spirituality is meant that measure of mind which says, after arriving at a certain place in Christian experience, I have arrived or I have attained; there is nothing beyond for me to achieve. There are multitudes of Christians content with the positional placement of justification who know nothing of the progressive power of sanctification. They are content with the center of Christianity but know nothing of the circumference of the Christian life. One grants that justification is a great experience, but an even greater series of advancing experiences await in the realms of God's dealings through our sanctification.

It was recently observed by an editorial writer in the *Toronto Globe* after an annual Orangemen's Day parade in that city that so many of the professed followers of King William have become stuffed shirts who will only walk if the weather is fine and who sit down to "walk" in their big cars bedecked with orange and blue banners. . . . They represent, figuratively, the fair-weather friends of God who literally sit down to walk in God's parade. They must be enticed to church by serenading them. Not in any sense can it be said of such Christians that they defend the faith by living for it. . . . This is one of the reasons why the church has been weakened. There are too many dress paraders in the ranks and not enough men and women who "walk worthy of their vocation." Parading is not enough. We've got to live for God and our faith. Too many of us are offenders of the faith instead of defenders of the faith.

Dress parading is another version of static Christian experience. This sort of thing is in for a rude awakening in Philippians where the theme and climax is reached in 3:13,14, "Brethren, I count not myself to have apprehended: but this one thing I do, forgetting those things which are behind, and reaching forth unto those things which are before, I press toward the mark for the prize of the high calling of God in Christ Jesus."

It is recorded that one of the Czars of Russia, walking in his palace park, came upon a sentry standing before a small patch of weeds. The Czar asked him what he was doing there. The sentry did not know; all he could say was that he had been

ordered to his post by the captain of the guard.
The Czar then sent his aide to ask the captain. But
the captain could only say that the regulations had
always called for a sentry at that particular spot.
His curiosity having been aroused, the Czar ordered
an investigation. No living man at the court could
remember a time when there had not been a sentry
at that post and none could say what he was guard-
ing. Finally, the archives were opened and after
a long search, the mystery was solved. The records
showed that the great Catherine had once planted
a rosebush in that plot of ground and a sentry had
been put there to see that no one trampled on it.
The rosebush died. No one had thought to cancel
the order for the sentry. For a hundred years the
spot where the rosebush had once been was watched
by men who did not know what they were watching. There are Christians who are serving tradition
in a similar manner. They are doing guard duty
over an old, faded, withered, dried-up experience
of twenty or thirty years. They have not gone a
step in advance. God is marching on. Christian
experience is progressive. Jesus said, "go," not
"stand." He said, "fight," not "guard." Let us then
adopt the theme of this book as the watchword of
our lives: "I press toward the mark for the prize
of the high calling of God in Christ Jesus."

The City of Philippi was a geographical frontier of the first century, an outpost at the periphery
of the empire. In the same manner the Epistle to

the Philippians contains the dimensions of a new spiritual frontier; of an ever-advancing Christian experience toward which its language entices the seeking soul.

OUTLINE OF PHILIPPIANS

A. THE CHRISTIAN'S SOURCE OF LIFE.
   Philippians 1:1-30.
   I. THE CHRISTIAN'S NEW POSITION. 1:1, 2.
   II. THE CHRISTIAN'S NEW ASSURANCE. 1:3-7.
   III. THE CHRISTIAN'S NEW LIFE. 1:8-11.
      1. A Life of Love. Verse 9.
      2. A Life of Discernment. Verse 10a.
      3. A Life of Sincerity. Verse 10b.
      4. A Life of Righteousness. Verse 11.
   IV. THE CHRISTIAN'S NEW ATTITUDE. 1:12-20.
      1. The Romans. Verse 13.
      2. The Christians. Verses 14-18.
      3. The Apostle. Verses 19, 20.
   V. THE CHRISTIAN'S NEW SECRET. 1:21-30.
      1. The New Secret of Death. Verses 21-26.
         (1) *The dissolution of a chemical.*
         (2) *The lifting of an anchor.*
         (3) *The striking of a tent.*
      2. The New Secret of Life. Verses 27-30.
         (1) *To stand fast.* Verse 27.
         (2) *To stand up.* Verses 28-30.

B. THE CHRISTIAN'S IDEAL FOR LIFE.
   Philippians 2:1-30.
   I. OUR PERSONAL CONDUCT. 2:1-4.

    1. The Basis of Christian Unity. Verses 1, 2.
      (1) *Of one love.*
      (2) *Of one accord.*
      (3) *Of one mind.*
    2. The Basis of Christian Conduct. Verses 3, 4.
      (1) *It was negative.* Verses 3, 4.
      (2) *It was positive.* Verses 3, 4.

II. THE PERSON OF CHRIST. 2:5-11.
    1. He Was Divine—His Pre-Existence. Verse 6.
    2. He Was Human—His Incarnation. Verse 7.
    3. He Was Obedient—His Atonement. Verse 8.
    4. He Was Exalted—His Resurrection and Ascension. Verse 9.
    5. He Is Supreme—His Return. Verses 10, 11.

III. THE CHRISTIAN'S SALVATION. 2:12,13.
    1. The Out-Worked Labor. Verse 12.
    2. The In-Worked Life. Verse 13.

IV. THE CHRISTIAN'S LIFE. 2:14-16.
    1. As an Illuminating Influence. Verse 15.
    2. As an Active Witness. Verse 16.

V. THE CHRISTIAN'S EXAMPLE. 2:17-30.
    1. Paul. Verses 17, 18.
    2. Timothy. Verses 19-23.
    3. Epaphroditus. Verses 24-30.

C. THE CHRISTIAN'S OBJECT IN LIFE.
Philippians 3:1-21.

  I. THE CHRISTIAN'S REJOICING. 3:1.

  II. THE CHRISTIAN'S PRESERVATION. 3:2, 3.

    1. A Warning Against False Christianity. Verse 2.

      (1) *"Beware of dogs."*

      (2) *"Beware of evil workers."*

      (3) *"Beware of the concision."*

    2. The Essentials of True Christianity. Verse 3.

      (1) *Its worship—"in the Spirit."*

      (2) *Its glory—"rejoice in Christ Jesus."*

      (3) *Its principle—"no confidence in the flesh."*

  III. THE CHRISTIAN'S TRUST. 3:4-7.

    1. Pride of Tradition. Verse 5.

    2. Pride of Birth. Verse 5.

    3. Pride of Position. Verse 5.

    4. Pride of Caste. Verse 5.

    5. Pride of Religion. Verse 5.

    6. Pride of Reputation. Verse 6.

    7. Pride of Character. Verse 6.

  IV. THE CHRISTIAN'S DESIRE. 3:8-11.

    1. The Desire to "win Christ." Verse 8.

    2. The Desire to be "found in Christ." Verse 9.

    3. The Desire to "know Him." Verses 10, 11.

(1) *To know Him in "the power of His resurrection."*
(2) *To know Him in "the fellowship of His sufferings."*
(3) *To know Him in "the conformation of His death."*

V. THE CHRISTIAN'S GOAL. 3:12-14.
1. "Forgetting those things which are behind." Verse 13.
2. "Reaching forth unto those things which are before." Verse 13.
3. "I press toward the mark for the prize of the high calling of God in Christ Jesus." Verse 14.

VI. THE CHRISTIAN'S WALK. 3:15-19.
1. The Extreme of Perfectionism. Verses 15, 16.
2. The Extreme of Antinomianism. Verses 17-19.

VII. THE CHRISTIAN'S HOPE. 3:20,21.
1. To Change Our Bodies. Verse 21.
2. To Subdue All Things. Verse 21.

D. THE CHRISTIAN'S PEACE IN LIFE. Philippians 4:1-23.

I. PEACE AND ITS RELATIONSHIP TO GOD. 4:1-4.
1. The Lord in the Midst. Verse 1.
2. The Lord in the Mind. Verses 2, 3.
3. The Lord in the Heart. Verse 4.

II. PEACE AND ITS RELATION TO PRAYER. 4:5-7.
1. The First Condition. Verse 5.

2. The Second Condition. Verse 6.
   (1) Prayer that begins without excessive care—*"Be careful for nothing."*
   (2) Prayer that prays for everything—*"in every thing by prayer and supplication."*
   (3) Prayer that is thankful—*"with thanksgiving."*
   (4) Prayer that is specific—*"let your requests be made known unto God."*
3. The Result. Verse 7.
   (1) It is *"the peace of God."*
   (2) It is peace *"which passeth all understanding."*
   (3) It is peace which *"keeps."*
III. PEACE AND ITS RELATION TO THE MIND. 4:8,9.
   1. Thinking. Verse 8.
      (1) *Because what we think we become.*
      (2) *Because our thoughts are the channel of the transforming grace of God.*
   2. Doing. Verse 9.
IV. PEACE AND ITS RELATION TO OUR CIRCUMSTANCES. 4:10-19.
   1. How to Be Satisfied Wherever You Are. Verses 10-12.
      (1) *"I have learned."* Verse 11.
      (2) *"I am instructed."* Verse 12.
   2. How to Be Strong for Whatever You Must Do. Verse 13.
      (1) *He can be "salt" and "light."*

  (2) *He can be a witness.*
  (3) *He can be fruitful.*
  (4) *He can maintain good works.*
  (5) *He can live without habitual sin.*

 3. How to be Supplied with Whatever You Need. Verses 14-19.

  (1) *Christian courtesy.* Verses 10, 14, 16.
  (2) *The purpose behind giving.* Verse 17.
  (3) *Giving and receiving.* Verse 15.
  (4) *The gift to Paul equivalent of a gift to God.* Verse 18.
  (5) *The gift to Paul an example of proper Christian relief.* Verses 14, 16.

V. SALUTATIONS OF FAREWELL. 4:20-23.

1

THE CHRISTIAN'S SOURCE OF LIFE

Philippians 1

THE SOURCE of the Christian's life is Jesus Christ. This is so stated in verse 21 which is the key to the truth of the chapter. "For to me to live is Christ . . ." Christianity is Christ. He is the heart of Christian life and the secret of an advancing Christian experience. It is a Christo-centric life. It is the spiritual biological fact of Christ living His life in us. We provide the human facilities and He provides the divine power.

There are six new relationships of the Christian to Christ in this chapter. To recognize and respect these relationships is to put ourself into the experiences of fullness and fruitfulness in living.

I. THE CHRISTIAN'S NEW POSITION. Verses 1, 2.

> "Paul and Timotheus, the servants of Jesus Christ, to all the saints in Christ Jesus which are at Philippi, with the bishops and deacons: Grace be unto you, and peace, from God our Father, and from the Lord Jesus Christ."

Everything in life, every measure of success, every pinnacle of attainment depends upon the position from which we begin our Christian lives. Our position will determine our condition. Where we begin will determine where we end. Where we start will determine how far we will go.

The position of the Christian is described here as being "in Christ." This is his spiritual identification. This is the source of his life and his righteousness. This is the launching platform for his assault on life. This is the eminence of character from which he begins his Christian experience.

These are days when recurring cries call upon us to save some element of our contemporary life. In one case it is civilization which needs to be saved. In another case it is democracy which we must save, or it is the American way of life; and to these we add Christianity, and demands are made upon us to save it in crusade fashion. What an unthinkable concept of Christianity this is we will see upon a moment's reflection. If Christianity is something which needs to be saved then it is something which can be lost. If it can be lost then it is a human factor which depends upon us; and if it depends upon us we cannot depend upon it. It becomes a false hope which will fail upon trial. Dr. Edward S. Woods, Bishop of Croydon, once said: "The impression too easily prevails that the major business of churchmen is to keep religion going. But that was not the way Christianity started. The impression the first Christians gave to the world was that religion kept them going." This is exactly true. Christianity is not a form which we must sustain but a force which sustains us.

This fact appears in the position into which all believers are placed by regeneration. They were *in* Christ while *at* Philippi. The *source* of their life was Christ while the *sphere* of their life was Philippi. What they would be as Philippians was determined by what they were as Christians. The influence and strength of life was not drawn from their Philippian circumstances, but rather from their Christian characters. Life for them would be a demonstration of the power of character over circumstances and heredity over environment.

Philippi was a Roman colony, the local seat of government for the world-powerful Roman empire. The presence of the Roman legate and the Roman army gave an atmosphere of power; but here also was a greater power, the power of the life of Jesus Christ. Caesar has gone but Christ is the reigning sovereign of contemporary life in the lives of millions of Christians. Philippi is gone but colonies of heaven exist wherever a Christian church is planted. No matter how inhospitable the soil or antagonistic the environment, the gates of hell will not prevail against these heavenly colonies.

The continuity and vitality of the church is guaranteed in the simple secret of Christianity. It is to be *in Christ* while being at Philippi, or London, or Los Angeles, or Singapore. Jesus Christ will make the difference in every human situation, whether in citizen or city. It is not transplantation to new environments which we need but transformation into new men. It is bringing Christ to our cities that will change those cities. It is bringing Christ to our homes that will change those homes. It is bringing Christ to our lives that will change those lives. It is when Jesus Christ is linked to our circumstances through regenerated character that His power can be brought to bear upon our life situations.

That there was a valid church at Philippi is evident from the addressees of the epistle. It was to saints with bishops and deacons, an evidence of a local church structure. It is sufficient comment to say that the saints were not a special company of people who had died and were canonized under ecclesiastical authority but the living members of the Philippian assembly. Their bishops or elders and deacons were local overseers and ministrants whose authorities and functions were apparently limited to individual congregations.

In the face of the evidence of a local church structure and a valid Christian church existing at this outpost of human power and exercising a transforming influence upon pagan culture, there is scant room for modern denunciations upon the part of fragmentary sects which seek to belittle church organization and denominational importance.

Lying within a combine of two words is a mighty truth. The words are a part of the salutation of verse 2: "Grace be unto you, and peace."

Grace and peace are the natural possession of our spiritual position. Grace is the cause and peace is the effect. They are divine characteristics invoked upon the Philippians and were to be for life in all the changing conditions that might exist under Roman rule. They are stabilizers of character to prevent fluctuation with political fortunes or economic conditions or adverse states of health.

With these qualities of grace and peace it would not be the case, as Thoreau once observed, of "men living lives of quiet desperation." The normality of Christian experience is not "quiet" or any other kind of desperation; it is the conquest of contemporary life through the grace of God which produces peace in all life's situations.

A man once stood beside a mighty redwood towering toward the skies. As he gazed with admiring wonder at its amazing size and height, he spoke to the tree as if it were a thing of intelligence. "O, Giant Sequoia," he said, "such bulk and altitude are not the creation of a day nor a year. You may have lived a thousand years. Have you anything to say to me?" As he listened, he thought he heard the tree reply: "Yes, I have lived a long time—a thousand years or more—and I have this to say to you: I have learned that all storms blow over. Life with me is the same as life with you. No matter how fierce the gales, how wild the tempest, they spend their day, and then the calm. While the tempests of life rage the atmosphere of life is to be peace."

All of this is confirmed in the second of the Christian's six new relationships to Christ.

II. The Christian's New Assurance. Verses 3-7.

> "I thank my God upon every remembrance of you, always in every prayer of mine for you all making request with joy, for your fellowship in the gospel from the first day until now; being confident of this very thing, that he which hath begun a good work in you will perform it until the day of Jesus Christ: Even as it is meet for me to think this of you all, because I have you in my heart; inasmuch as both in my bonds, and in the defence and confirmation of the gospel, ye all are partakers of my grace."

Imbedded in these words to an ancient church lies the source of much happiness and usefulness. They are found in this sentiment, "remembrance of you." Personal relations are the key to almost everything in the world. People like to be remembered. Paul remembers the Philippians with gratitude to God. It was with compliment and not complaint. Few today display this quality of graciousness to the extent that it should be current in our Christian relationships.

Public relations is an important part of Christian experience. The simplest secret of a good public relation is to remember others instead of thinking of ourselves. If you want people to like you all you need to do is to like them. You will be interesting to others when you are interested in them.

The dominant assurance here is that Christian experience has an ultimate goal. It is found in the words of verse 6, "Being confident of this very thing, that he which hath begun a good work in you will perform it until the day of Jesus Christ." This gives meaning and purpose to life and the only life with such an assured purpose is the Christian life. It alone is worth living because it alone can promise an adequate goal for our faith and effort.

We are advancing and moving on to a grand climax, a great conclusion and a glorious consummation. This is described elsewhere in Scripture as likeness to Jesus Christ. The process by which we will be brought to this likeness is spoken of as a "good work."

The performer and "finisher" of this good work is God. Paul's confident assurance is in God's "finishiative" as well as God's initiative. He is the author and finisher of our faith. In the work of God since the creative beginning you will find everything completed and finished. This is not true of man for in his working areas you find unfinished canvases, unfinished statues, unfinished songs, unfinished books and unfinished buildings. But nowhere in God's workshops can you find an unfinished sun or star or flower; and this record of finishiative assures us that the God who is now working in redemptive grace in the lives of men is working to the same purpose of completion and perfection.

The "nature" of this work is redemptive. The God of creation is now the God of redemption. He who made planets is now making men; and the "good work" in which God is now occupied is the making of men according to the pattern likeness of Jesus Christ.

Redemption has two aspects. The first aspect is regenerative when God takes a sinner and regenerates him by the power of His grace, giving him a place in his divine family, communicating to him a divine nature and making him a new creature. The second aspect is that of development and is what this epistle emphasizes in terms of advancement and personal progress. It is that aspect that is technically known as sanctification, when God undertakes to work out in us what Christ worked out for us.

The "energy" of this good work is grace. Grace is God's energy or manner of dealing with our spiritual natures. It is not an impractical thing as we are in danger of thinking. Power in creative energy was God's manner of producing the creation. Grace is the form or manifestation of that mighty power or energy in making new men.

The "extent" of this good work is indicated in the word "perform" which means to complete, perfect or finish. The historical phase of redemption was completed on the Cross. The personal and continuing phase of redemption will be perfected or completed at Christ's second coming. It will be a continuous process up to and including that event. What began in history is finished in prophecy. There is a commencement, a course and a consummation in the Christian life.

It should be noted that the believer is one who is perfect in his position while being made perfect in his condition. His position is illustrated by what the Philippian Christians were "in Christ." His condition is to be demonstrated by what these same Philippian Christians were to be like "at Philippi." In union we are perfect while in communion we are being perfected. No one can be united to God except the basis of union be justification, perfect standing; whereas the relationship of communion carries sanctifying powers that admit of that which is being perfected in human behavior while constantly progressing in the ideal of perfection.

Here is the point of reconciliation between what God does for us and what we must do for ourselves. The position we occupy "in Christ" is by God's work of grace apart from human merit and effort. But the kind of life we live in our individual Philippiis is determined by our progress in grace which is a part of the finishing work which is now going on. The extent of progress is determined by our application of the means of grace which God makes available to our lives. Included in these means of grace are the indwelling Holy Spirit, the use of God's Word, the exercise of prayer, Christian worship and Christian fellowship.

The "terminus" of this good work is described as the "day of Jesus Christ." This does not mean the day of our death, for the work of grace goes beyond that day to the "day of Jesus Christ." Nor does this mean that grace operates in the state of death in the form of purgatorial fires. It does mean that whatever unfinished business may have remained at the time of our death will be transacted at the Judgment Seat of Christ which is an eschatological event incident to those events related to Christ's advent.

By all these things from the "finisher" of this good work to the "terminus" of it we observe that Christian experience is not a religious event of nebulous nature or purpose. It is God's definitive purpose for human life in which Christians are brought to the character likeness of Jesus Christ. They are then scheduled to participate in the ultimate purposes of grace at the end of this perfecting progress, a participation which will extend through eternal ages.

In the construction of a new church building it was necessary to have steel beams of such length and specifications that they had to be rolled and fabricated in eastern mills and shipped by boat to California. The steel fabricators insisted on some payment with the order and the contractor insisted on some valid assurance that after receiving payment they would faithfully fulfill their contract. This was given in the form of a Faithful Performance Bond. A bonding company agreed to be surety for the steel company to the amount of the order to assure the faithful performance of its contract.

The Scripture we have been dealing with sets forth a contractual arrangement in which "He which hath begun a good work in you will perform it until the day of Jesus Christ." This is God's contract with us and the Holy Spirit is God's Faithful Performance Bond that this contract will be faithfully executed. ". . . Ye were sealed with that holy Spirit of promise, which is the earnest [pledge money] of our inheritance until the redemption of the purchased possession" (Eph. 1:13,14).

III. THE CHRISTIAN'S NEW LIFE. Verses 8-11.

"For God is my record, how greatly I long after you all in the bowels of Jesus Christ. And this I pray, that your love may abound yet more and more in knowledge and in all judgment; that ye may approve things that are excellent; that ye may be sincere and without offence till the day of Christ; being filled with the fruits of righteousness, which are by Jesus Christ, unto the glory and praise of God."

The elements of this new life are presented in the form of Paul's prayer for the Philippians. This prayer is voiced out of deep affection, an affection stated in the most expressive way an oriental could speak, for Paul says, "I long after you all in the bowels of Jesus Christ." This area was considered by the ancients to be the seat of the affections. They understood this because deep emotional reactions registered in the area of this center of our sympathetic nervous system with physical sensations of shock and nausea.

Paul was voicing his prayer for their lives not just in his love but with the deepest of all affection, the love of Jesus Christ.

It was a prayer for:

1. A Life of Love. Verse 9.

> "And this I pray, that your love may abound yet more and more in knowledge and in all judgment."

This is the highest form of life but it is also the highest form of love for Paul prays for a love which has in it the elements of knowledge and good judgment. Way's translation of this entire passage speaks of it as a love that rises "higher and higher to its fullest development in recognition of the truth and in a comprehensive grasp of its application, thus furnishing you with a sure test of what is true excellence, so that you may remain untainted by error, unstumbling amidst obstacles, till the day of Messiah's appearing, bearing the while a full harvest of righteousness, attained through Jesus our Messiah and redounding to the praise and glory of God."

This prayer is for a life filled and permeated by such love because a matured Christian love is the way to the most sensitive virtues and to the highest knowledge. We say of love that it is blind. It is when it is fancied affection, but here is a love which brings the cognition of divine truth and the activity of the highest moral perceptions. Through it we enter the most exciting and exhilarating experiences of life for love is the highest expression of life.

2. A Life of Discernment. Verse 10a.

"That ye may approve things that are excellent."

Possessed of such love the Christian would acquire a moral discernment which enables him to judge between right and wrong, truth and error. Where there is real love there is a deep moral sensitiveness. Love provides its own defenses against defection.

A fully developed love means the highest development of personality which in turn means maturity. With maturity comes discernment and with discernment these Philippians would "remain untainted by error, unstumbling amidst obstacles."

3. A Life of Sincerity. Verse 10b.

"That ye may be sincere and without offence till the day of Christ."

"Sincere" is derived from a Latin expression meaning to be "without wax." Wood might be filled with wax to conceal its flaws. A sculptor's work might be filled with wax to conceal his lack of skill.

Its scriptural equivalent is to be pure and unsullied.

Sincerity is being transparent. You will be known on the outside for what you are on the inside. There will be moral transparency so that one can be seen through and through, whereas the opposite is true of the hypocrite who wears a second face.

Sincerity is being true. Lincoln said, "I am not bound to win, but I am bound to be true. I am not bound to succeed, but I am bound to live up to what light I have. I must stand with anybody who stands right; stand with him while he is right and part with him when he goes wrong."

Sincerity is being real. In a radio play given during the last war by a group of actors known as the Free Company, one of the players said to a companion actor, "You sound like a preacher, only it sounds real." Is it so insincere a characteristic of preachers and their preaching that they do not sound real but are only the mechanical sounding boards of religious creeds and languages? Or is this the calumnious remark of a cheap critic. Let us be sure we are real and sound like it as well.

The concomitant of sincerity is to be "without offence." In this case it means that Paul is praying for a life that has sincerity plus discernment and love which leads to that condition where it does not cause others to stumble. It is without the offending inconsistencies that bring Christ's cause into shame and disrepute.

4. A Life of Righteousness. Verse 11.

"Being filled with the fruits of righteousness, which
are by Jesus Christ, unto the glory and praise of
God."

The "fruits of righteousness" are to be distinguished from the fruits of faith. The fruits of faith
are the result of service and activity. The fruits of
righteousness are the result of character which in
this case is dominated by love. It is what comes because of what we are rather than because of what
we do.

Love is the root while righteousness is the fruit.
The root is idealistic. The fruit is realistic. This
fruit of righteousness is the practical effect of the
indwelling Christ. These attainments are but the
extension of His life, His power, His grace and His
character through the Christian.

This concludes Paul's prayer for love, the highest development of Christian character to be followed by the highest achievements of Christian
life. Love is the guarantee of the best life.

"There was a time when in my daily prayer
I asked for all the things I deemed most fair,
And necessary to my life — success,
Riches, of course, and ease and happiness;
A host of friends, a home without alloy;
A primrose path of luxury and joy,
Social distinction and enough of fame
To leave behind a well-remembered name.

Ambition ruled my life. I longed to do great things,
Great things, that all my little world might view
And whisper, 'Wonderful!' Ah, patient God,
How blind we are, until Thy shepherd's rod
Of tender chastening, gently leads us on
To better things!
Ah, Love Divine, how empty was that prayer
Of other days! That which was once so fair,
Those flimsy baubles which the world calls joys,
Are nothing to me but broken toys,
Outlived, out-grown, I thank Thee that I know
Those much-desired dreams of long ago
Like butterflies have had their summer's day
Of brief enchantment, and have gone. I pray
For better things, Thou knowest. God above
My one desire now — Teach me to love."

IV. THE CHRISTIAN'S NEW ATTITUDE. Verses 12-20.

"But I would ye should understand, brethren, that
the things which happened unto me have fallen
out rather unto the furtherance of the gospel; So
that my bonds in Christ are manifest in all the
palace, and in all other places; And many of the
brethren in the Lord, waxing confident by my
bonds, are much more bold to speak the word
without fear. Some indeed preach Christ even of
envy and strife; and some also of good will: The
one preach Christ of contention, not sincerely, supposing to add affliction to my bonds: But the other
of love, knowing that I am set for the defence of
the gospel. What then? notwithstanding, every
way, whether in pretence, or in truth, Christ is
preached; and I therein do rejoice, yea, and will
rejoice. For I know that this shall turn to my sal-

vation through your prayer, and the supply of the
Spirit of Jesus Christ, According to my earnest
expectation and my hope, that in nothing I shall
be ashamed, but that with all boldness, as always,
so now also Christ shall be magnified in my body,
whether it be by life, or by death."

What appears here has reference to Paul's imprisonment in Rome. It is in fact Paul's philosophy
of misfortune. He undertakes to explain a situation
which seemed incompatible with Christian faith.
There were Philippians who lamented the imprisonment. In fact, they were more troubled over Paul's
incarceration than he was. It is often true that those
who watch others suffer are more troubled with the
problem of suffering than the sufferers themselves.
The loudest complainers against God's justice and
goodness are the watchers—not the sufferers. The
by-standers are the chief critics of God. The ob-
servers are the most vocal. It was true in the classic
case of Job. Not until his would-be comforters began to complain did Job feel his experience so keen-
ly. And Job's problem was not resolved, as his
counselors expected, by an explanation but rather
by an experience of God.

The law of contrast operates in God's dealings
with us. Only those who have experienced the bitter
can appreciate the sweet. There is something in an
experience which can never be conveyed in a philo-
sophical or theological explanation. If this were not

true men could learn life by collecting ideas about it. The fact is, life is something which we come to understand by living rather than learning.

The attitude of the Christian to life concerns God's purpose. In this attitude misfortune can serve a good purpose as Paul declares in verse 12, "But I would ye should understand, brethren, that the things which happened unto me have fallen out rather unto the furtherance of the gospel." This good thing which "happened unto me" was not the chance effect of a situation or the fortuitous result of an accident. It was a part of the divine management of Paul's life and as a result of his bonds there was an effect which could not have been achieved in any other way.

What happened to Paul in his imprisonment appeared to be a deathblow to the hopes of the pitifully small minority of Christians then in the world, for Paul was the greatest evangelizing force of the Christian community. But Paul's attitude was different. He saw an advantage and a profit they did not see. He said, "The things which happened unto me have fallen out rather unto the furtherance of the gospel," or as the Revised Standard Version puts it, "has really served to advance the gospel." What seemed to sight to be a retardation was to faith and fact an acceleration. What seemed to hinder really served to help. What seemed to prevent in actual fact promoted. What appeared to be a misfortune proved to be a blessing.

The providential effect of the apostle's imprisonment was in three areas.

1. The Romans. Verse 13.

> "So that my bonds in Christ are manifest in all the palace, and in all other places."

The advantage effected by the imprisonment served to take Paul out of anonymity and comparative obscurity and make him the object of public notice in the praetorium or barracks of the imperial bodyguard and in "all other places." Otherwise Paul's sphere of influence might have been confined to the members of the local Christian community. But now he was able to reach the imperial guards, slaves, courtiers and the population of Rome generally.

The imprisonment was not in the traditional dungeon in convict isolation, for Paul was a special prisoner and a prize to be held with care; so he was quartered in the praetorium with a praetorian always present as his custodian. He was chained to successive shifts of these guards to whom he witnessed and when they were relieved returned to the barracks with the message. The apparent result was a revival in the imperial army.

Besides Paul's witness to the soldiers countless civilians had access to his prison quarters and Paul preached to them without hindrance, so that many were converted and carried the message to the civilian population of Rome. The result was out of all proportion to the disadvantage suffered by the apostle, for the name of Christ and the message of the gospel were carried empire-wide in a manner, and in such time, as could not be effected under any other circumstances than through the apparent calamity of Paul's imprisonment. No wonder Paul could so confidently and triumphantly say, "I would ye should understand, brethren, that the things which happened unto me have fallen out rather unto the furtherance of the gospel."

The occasion of our particular misfortune may not be either prisons or chains but it could be the walls of restricting circumstances and the providential chains of disability. One may be chained to a sickbed or others to a wheel chair, a kitchen, or limited by economic restrictions, or swallowed up in an obscure place; and it could seem to these under such incarcerating limitations that life can serve no useful purpose. But the difference between making these conditions an advantage or a disadvantage is solely up to us. It is the difference of attitude. It is the difference of faith. It is the difference between a crossroad of the world or a bypath of obscurity; and it is our attitude that makes just this difference.

Paul saw the advantage in his imprisonment to his mission in life and not to his personal feelings and he made the most of it. We, too, could see that "the difficulty with which we are now contending, the uncongenial people and the uncomfortable surroundings that so distress and apparently hinder us are just a providential pulpit and congregation which God has given us for the purpose of reaching people we could reach in no other way and teaching or learning lessons that could only thus be exemplified."

Personal resistance to reversals in fortune, occasions of mistreatment and experience of ill health result in defeating the purpose of an intelligent divine providence which is working to an over-all plan. We can miss some of the richest blessings and greatest opportunities simply because we expect every day of our lives to be filled with the comfortable experience we enjoy. Life has its prisons as well as its palaces, its restrictions as well as its liberties, its setbacks as well as its onsets. To accept this is to take a new attitude to life which will be fruitful in great blessing.

There was another area affected by Paul's imprisonment.

2. The Christians. Verses 14-18.

"And many of the brethren in the Lord, waxing confident by my bonds, are much more bold to speak the word without fear. Some indeed preach Christ even of envy and strife; and some also of good will: The one preach Christ of contention, not sincerely, supposing to add affliction to my bonds: But the other of love, knowing that I am set for the defence of the gospel. What then? notwithstanding, every way, whether in pretence, or in truth, Christ is preached; and I therein do rejoice, yea, and will rejoice."

Paul's fortitude of attitude and resistance of faith made Christians in Rome courageous. They were emboldened and reassured by Paul's example and fought fearlessly in their difficult surroundings. They were bold to "speak the word without fear" and converts were multiplied to the cause of Christ.

Who can tell how extensive our influence can be when we are faithful to Christ. Perhaps even now your own noble and courageous battle is giving reassurance and confidence to someone who is watching you.

But not all at Rome were preaching Christ from pure and unselfish motive. Some were doing it from jealousy, some with strife and factiousness, some in an attempt to aggravate Paul's imprisonment and consequently embarrass and harass him and some were doing it from a competitive party spirit. These latter were members of an anti-Pauline party of Judaizers who sought to fasten the restrictions of legalism upon Christian believers. They endeavored to set up the Christian faith in terms of Old Testament law and practice; and throughout Rome as well as Asia and Greece they "exercised an immoral, hostile opposition to the apostle and his gospel" Meyer's Commentary).

Regardless of the opposition of the Judaizing party, Paul rejoiced in the preaching of Christ because whatever the ulterior motive, it was Christ who was preached. It was an advantage to the cause of Christ in the long run because the mere presentation of His name, whether in truth or pretence, brought Him to the attention of the pagan world. Paul is expressing the conviction that God overrules and overcomes the strife, envy, hypocrisy, and contention that enter the human factors of God's work.

We who have intimate relation to God's work are frequently faced with the inconsistencies, weaknesses and sometimes sinfulness of those who are engaged in this work, reminding us that this treasure is indeed held in earthen vessels. But a sovereign God interposes His power to bless the truth and has given such inherent resilience to the gospel which may be channeled through an unfit and unworthy instrument that it succeeds in spite of the channel. We must fall back upon the conviction that God blesses the message in spite of the messenger.

The ultimate victory will surely and certainly come to those who hold the truth in its purity and live Christ in sincerity, no matter what the human shortcomings of other proponents may be.

Paul's generous attitude, free from intolerance, is beautiful to behold: "Notwithstanding, every way, whether in pretence, or in truth, Christ is preached; and I therein do rejoice, yea, and will rejoice." Paul rejoiced because Christ was set forth and He is the primary fact of the gospel. Whatever else was wrong this was right. However else the true meaning of Christianity was distorted Christ was exalted.

We must not miss the fact, however, that Paul's tolerance was not an endorsement of this Judaistic error. He rejoiced in what truth was present but did not compromise with the error. He could see that good could come in spite of the system rather than because of the system. The lesson is plain for us. There is a place for an intelligent and forebearing tolerance, but such tolerance is not a blindfold against either evil or error. God can overrule certain things to accomplish His purpose. In that case we should be content with the overruling providence of God instead of spending our time in the hatred of intolerance.

We, however, may be as guilty of the party spirit in other ways as any falsifier of the gospel. Ours may be the spirit of those who think the gospel must be preached through the mould of our human ideas. But we should remember that the world is made up of many types of people. Some can be reached only through an emotional approach; others only through a logical approach. Some insist on simplicity; others wish the oratory of Apollos. The main thing is that Christ be preached in His New Testament proportions.

3. The Apostle. Verses 19, 20.

"For I know that this shall turn to my salvation through your prayer, and the supply of the Spirit of Jesus Christ, according to my earnest expecta-

tion and my hope, that in nothing I shall be
ashamed, but that with all boldness, as always, so
now also Christ shall be magnified in my body,
whether it be by life, or by death."

Enduring imprisonment outside the Christian
community and facing opposition inside, Paul nevertheless held an optimistic view of the final outcome.
He says in verse 19, "I know that this shall turn to my
salvation through your prayer, and the supply of the
Spirit of Jesus Christ." Christianity will triumph in
spite of both the weakness of its proponents and the
opposition of its opponents. It will triumph because
it is not we who keep Christianity going but Christ.
It is the expression and extension of the life of Jesus
Christ and He cannot fail since He is sovereign, although necessarily working through human instruments and incidents.

There is an interrelation and interdependence
involved in the success of our Christian cause that
we must not overlook. Paul states it in these words:
"I know that this shall turn to my salvation through
your prayer, and the supply of the Spirit of Jesus
Christ." Paul's dependence for success was both
human and divine. He needed the prayers of the
Philippians and he needed the divine help of the
Spirit. Both are essential. This interlocking relation exists for all Christians. We must have each
other and prayer is the link between us. This is
illustrated from the last war. An American soldier

wounded on a battlefield in the Far East owes his life to the Japanese scientist, Kitasato, who isolated the bacillus of tetanus. A Russian soldier saved by a blood transfusion is indebted to Landsteiner, an Austrian. A German is shielded from typhoid fever with the help of a Russian, Metchnikoff. A Dutch marine in the East Indies is protected from malaria because of the experiments of an Italian, Grassi; while a British aviator in North Africa escapes death from surgical infection because a Frenchman, Pasteur, and a German, Koch, elaborated a new technique. In peace as in war we are all of us beneficiaries of contributions to knowledge contributed by every nation in the world. Our children are guarded from diphtheria by what a Japanese and a German did; they are protected from smallpox by an Englishman's work; they are saved from rabies because of a Frenchman; they are cured of pellagra through the researches of an Austrian. The Christians of Germany needed the prayers, benevolences and good will of their fellow believers in England. The believers of Japan needed the prayers of those in America. There is a fellowship that goes beyond nationality and erases geography and even ignores declarations of war. Christianity is a communion of people in which "there is neither Greek nor Jew, circumcision nor uncircumcision, Barbarian, Scythian, bond nor free: but Christ is all and in all" and we are all in Christ.

The apostle expresses a contagious optimism concerning the final and ultimate effect of his own Christian service, "According to my earnest expectation and my hope, that in nothing I shall be ashamed, but that with all boldness, as always, so now also Christ shall be magnified in my body, whether it be by life, or by death." The reason for this confidence arises from the manner of his own life as well as the prayers of the Philippians and divine help as previously expressed. The depth of his own devotion is seen in the fact that "Christ shall be magnified in my body, whether it be by life, or by death." It was to be a magnification of Christ in Paul's body by life or by death. This meant the total involvement of Paul. It was to be on every day and not merely Sunday. It was to be in every place and not just in the temple.

The realization of Paul's intention to so completely magnify Christ lies in the fact that his body was the temple of the Holy Spirit and he proposed to glorify God in that which was His temple. It was not his intention to glorify the body, but God in the body; nor was it intended that he would mortify the flesh, but sins in the flesh. Likewise these bodies are to become the workshop of the Holy Carpenter of Nazareth. They are to be the earthly frames for heavenly pictures. They are to be vessels of clay that hold priceless treasure. The intent of these things can only be realized as we present our bodies to be living sacrifices.

> "I free myself from all belief
> That I am bound by pain or grief;
> The things that others do and say
> Erect no barriers in my way.
> All past mistakes I leave behind,
> New courage, hope and joy I find
> As I begin this day.
> I free myself from lack of fear,
> The habits formed in yesteryear,
> Old grievances are laid away
> And with a hopeful heart I pray
> That in my body, soul and mind
> A worthy channel God will find
> To do His work, this day."

It is conceivable that we can magnify Christ by life, but what does it mean "by death"? Death cuts off life and stops usefulness. But in every life lived for Christ, life and death are different phases of the same life. There is a way to live while living so that we may go on living after death. There is a consecration to life which makes death but an incident in passage from time to eternity and robs it of all its seeming conclusiveness. There is a way also to die that calls attention to life in such a manner that others will want it.

While James is the only apostle whose actual death is recorded in Scripture, tradition tells us that all the apostles died martyrs' deaths. James, the brother of John, slain by Herod's sword; Philip, crucified at Heliopolis in Phrygia; James the less, clubbed to death in Jerusalem; Andrew, crucified at Edessa; Thomas, thrust through with a spear in India; Simon, the Zealot, crucified in Briton; Thaddeus, crucified at Edessa; Bartholomew, beaten and crucified in India; Peter, crucified at Rome (with his head down, because, according to tradition, he deemed himself unworthy to die in the same manner as his Lord); John, exiled to Patmos, and believed to have been horribly martyred by being cast into boiling oil; Matthew, beheaded in Ethiopia; Paul, the apostle born out of due time, beheaded at Rome, following his imprisonment. These were all succeeded by a glorious succession of heroes of the faith including the Huguenots of France and the Covenanters of Scotland.

Against these noble traditions of deaths for Christ there is such an experience as a martyr's life in which men have died inwardly to self and selfishness and have discovered a new life of power and fruitfulness.

When an English soldier was being commiserated upon the loss of an arm in battle, he proudly replied, "I did not lose it: I gave it." And when we give our lives, our health, our youth, our years, our time and our money to Christ we forestall any comment on losing our lives, for we have already given them in happy and joyful surrender so that Christ shall be magnified whether by life or by death.

In a similar approach to life's pressing and perpetual problems we will find our answers in this same spirit of surrender as we give God what He may providentially intend to take.

Dr. W. E. Sangster writes that a member of his congregation came to his door one day in deep distress. Her daughter had been admitted to an eye clinic. The disease was more vicious than anyone had guessed and, on the day when the visitor stumbled up the parsonage doorsteps, the blow had fallen. The doctor's verdict had been given; the girl would be blind in a month. The doctor thought it best that the mother break the news to her daughter. Now the mother was passing the responsibility on to Dr. Sangster. He went, he said, with faltering footsteps to the hospital, and as he entered the door the girl turned her failing eyes toward him. He talked of trivialities, he said, sparring for an opening, and half afraid that she would guess the worst before he told her, and she did. For suddenly she cried: "Oh, I believe that God is going to take my sight away." This was an hour of "perpetual agony." "Jessie, I wouldn't let Him do it," begged Sangster. "Do what?" she asked. "Take my sight away." She begged him to explain, and he asked if she thought that in three weeks or a month she could pray a prayer like this: "Father, if for any reason known to Thee I must lose my sight, I will not let it be taken from me. I will give it to Thee." Some days later she reached out and found his hand and said that she couldn't live without light. But in three weeks, he said, she prayed that prayer—just as the last glimmer of day vanished from her sight. And with the prayer came peace and power.

V. THE CHRISTIAN'S NEW SECRET. Verses 21-30.

1. The New Secret of Death. Verses 21-26.

"For to me to live is Christ, and to die is gain. But if I live in the flesh, this is the fruit of my labour: yet what I shall choose I wot not. For I am in a strait betwixt two, having a desire to depart, and to be with Christ; which is far better: Nevertheless to abide in the flesh is more needful for you. And having this confidence, I know that I shall abide and continue with you all for your furtherance and joy of faith; that your rejoicing may be more abundant in Jesus Christ for me by my coming to you again."

The Christian's secret links both life and death. Life is Christ and death is gain. This is the key to a full and undefeated life. For the Christian living is Christ because He is the source and secret of life. Likewise dying is gain because in dying we gain the immediate presence of Christ. Death can only be gain when we live for Christ. Otherwise it is loss.

Luther, commenting upon Paul's conclusive utterance at this point says, "Christus ist mein leben." This is the essential fact of Christian doctrine and theology. Christ is at the center and all Christian life is in Him. He determines the nature

of Christian experience. As bird-life makes birds
and plant-life makes plants and animal-life makes
animals and human-life makes humans, so Christ-
life makes Christians. This Christian life is life
organic and not religious mechanics. It is response
to an inner life and not stimulation by an outer
cause.

If we cannot say, "For to me to live is Christ,
and to die is gain," then we live only to die. This
is so because the only one who can give meaning
and purpose to life is Christ. Remove Him from
this sentence and it will record a tragedy. Take
out the word "Christ" and you must remove the
word "gain" with the two qualifying words "and"
and "is"; and all you have left is, "For to me to live
is . . . to die." Life has only the meaning of death
when Christ is absent, for death is at its end no
matter what temporary gains have been achieved.

Just what sort of gain is death? Paul explains
it in verse 23: "For I am in a strait betwixt two,
having a desire to depart, and to be with Christ;
which is far better." He faced a dilemma posed by
duty and desire. Duty demanded that he remain
in the flesh and labor for those who needed his
ministry. Desire prompted him to depart to be
with Christ which he conceived as a "far better"
experience.

What a place heaven must be when it is described as "far better!" Here Paul was not expressing wishful thinking. He was talking from experi-

ence for he had already had a preview of a Christian's death. He had been previously "caught up" and had experienced what he described as "not lawful [possible] for a man to utter."

Death for Paul was a certainty: not an uncertainty. It was conscious existence: not unconscious oblivion. It was to be "with Christ": not in a grave. It was "far better": not dreadful or tragic. It was a part of life: not the conclusion to life. It was a beginning: not an ending. It was a commencement: not ceasing to be. Yes, it was life on a far better and grander scale.

The Christian concept of death is contained in a single word as employed by Paul—the word "depart." It has at least three meanings.

(1) *The dissolution of a chemical.*

In the case of a chemical compound in the form of a tablet it will dissolve when dropped into water. In dissolving it disappears but is not destroyed. Its form is changed from a solid to a liquid by the catalytic agency of water but its substance remains the same. When the Christian dies he disappears and the form of his life changes from a physical manifestation through a body to a spiritual manifestation.

(2) *The lifting of an anchor*

Anchors are lifted for ships about to get under way. When the vessel and its human cargo disappears across the horizon it is not lost, only out of sight. It exchanges one shore for another: one land for another. When a Christian dies death severs the ties which anchor him to this world and he departs for another land called heaven and another life described as "far better."

(3) *The striking of a tent.*

When journeys are resumed after sleep, tents are struck or taken down and travel continues. For a Christian life is a pilgrimage and his body is a tabernacle or tent. It is a temporary and ephemeral habitation. When death comes the tent of his body is struck and laid aside while the spirit moves into a more permanent residence. "For we know that if our earthly house of this tabernacle were dissolved, we have a building of God, an house not made with hands, eternal in the heavens" (II Cor. 5:1).

In these descriptions of death for a Christian it is a departure that means a meeting again; a separation that means a reunion; an exodus that means an entrance; a dissolution that means a new form of life. The wife of a Korean missionary lay dying. Her husband looked with love's solicitation into her face and heard her say, "Dear, don't feel too bad when I am gone. Don't feel impatient with God. Remember you will have me again." A month later his only son lay dying. "Daddy," he said, "I am going to mother. I need her so much. Don't feel too bad when I am gone. Remember, you will have mother and me again."

"Why be afraid of death, as though your life were breath?
Death but anoints your eyes with clay. O glad surprise!
Why should you be forlorn? Death only husks the corn.
Why should you fear to meet the thresher of the wheat?
Is sleep a thing to dread? Yet sleeping you are dead
Till you awake and rise, here, or beyond the skies.
Why should it be a wrench to leave yon wooden bench?
Why not, with happy shout, run home when school is out?
The dear ones left behind? Oh, foolish one and blind!
A day and you will meet — a night and you will greet.
This is the death of death to breathe away a breath
And know the end of strife, and taste the deathless life,
And joy without a fear, and smile without a tear;
And work, nor care to rest, and find the last the best."
— Babcock.

2. The New Secret of Life. Verses 27-30.

"Only let your conversation be as it becometh the gospel of Christ: that whether I come and see you, or else be absent, I may hear of your affairs, that ye stand fast in one spirit, with one mind striving together for the faith of the gospel; and in nothing terrified by your adversaries: which is to them an evident token of perdition, but to you of salvation, and that of God. For unto you it is given in the behalf of Christ, not only to believe on him, but also to suffer for his sake; having the same conflict which ye saw in me, and now hear to be in me."

The Christian life not only gives a new view of death: but death gives a new view of life. This new view of life refers to the Christian's obligation to make the most of life in view of the fleetness of time as well as passing of opportunity.

Paul uses the particularly important word "conversation." It is not conversation in the sense of language, but life. It means citizenship and originates with a word from which we get "politics." They are being instructed to act in line with their new citizenship for they are citizens of the Kingdom of heaven. What they were to be as citizens of Philippi was determined by their heavenly citizenship. What they were as Philippians was determined by what they were as Christians. And all this means that as the citizens of heaven they would be better citizens of Philippi. Christianity is not political but ethical and it enjoins upon each of us a faithful earthly citizenship on an ethical pattern.

Christianity not only improves character but because of that improvement of character improves our conduct as citizens, neighbors, parents, children, businessmen, employees, employers and students.

This manner of citizenship life is to be "as becometh the gospel of Christ." It is to be worthy of the gospel or fitting and proper. We often speak of people wearing clothes becoming to them. We mean that their clothes are worthy of face and form so as to present them to their best advantage. Their clothes are consistent with their physical make-up and consequently enhance their appearance. This is what the Bible means elsewhere when it says, "that they may adorn the doctrine of God our Saviour in all things" (Titus 2:10).

Two ways are suggested by which this new citizenship may adorn the doctrine of God in a fitting and worthy manner.

(1) To Stand Fast. Verse 27.

> "Only let your conversation be as it becometh the gospel of Christ: that whether I come and see you, or else be absent, I may hear of your affairs, that ye stand fast in one spirit, with one mind striving together for the faith of the gospel."

They were to stand together and strive together. Standing meant their spiritual posture while striving meant their spiritual action. It requires both posture and action. It meant the preservation of unity and the preservation of the faith.

This standing fast was to be done with the same intensity of effort that is true of athletic contests because Paul has borrowed a term from athletic competition when he uses the words "striving together." In this intense spirit of competition they were to maintain a united front and a united faith.

(2) To Stand Up. Verses 28-30.

> "And in nothing terrified by your adversaries: which is to them an evident token of perdition, but to you of salvation, and that of God. For unto you it is given in the behalf of Christ, not only to believe on him, but also to suffer for his sake; having the same conflict which ye saw in me, and now hear to be in me."

This meant the display of courage in the face of opposition and difficulty. They would be required to stand up as Christian bipeds and face both adversary and adversity. They would not only have to believe something intensely but suffer acutely for what they believed.

Few who read these words have suffered in the manner or to the measure of the Philippians but faith has its price. It may not now be the price of blood and physical deprivations, but it will always be the price of confession, sincerity, obedience, separation and identification.

Being a Christian does not mean exemption from suffering, sorrow, adversity, disappointment or hardship. It is not a way to get out of difficulty but a way to get on in difficulty. It is not an easy life, but it is the best life. It is the only life which can give you purpose and power for living.

"Caesar said, 'We will soon root up this Christianity. Off with their heads!' The different governors hastened one after another of the disciples to death; but the more they persecuted them, the more they multiplied. The proconsuls had orders to destroy Christians: the more they hunted them, the more Christians there were, until, at last, men pressed to the judgment seat and asked to be permitted to die for Christ. They invented torments; they dragged saints at the heels of wild horses; they laid them upon red-hot gridirons; they pulled off the skin from their flesh piece by piece; they were sawn asunder; they were wrapped up in skins, and daubed with pitch, and set in Nero's gardens at night to burn; they were left to rot in dungeons; they were made a spectacle to all men in the amphitheatre; the bears hugged them to death; the lions tore them to pieces; the wild bulls tossed them upon their horns; and yet Christianity spread. All the swords of the legionnaires which had put the armies of all nations to route, and overcame the invincible and the savage Briton, could not withstand the feebleness of Christianity; for the weakness of God is mightier than men."

The Christian church has been established and spread abroad by suffering in the collective church. But what is collective is also individual and individual suffering has a place in the program of living. Individual possession means individual participation in the divine disciplines. The future is made in the present. We cannot become greater or better than what we allow God to do in us, for us or through us. God cannot get depth out of a shallow life. Gold cannot be had except by fire. Sap cannot flow except by a wound. One cannot drink grapes. And as Oswald Chambers observes, "God can never make us wine if we object to the fingers He uses to crush us with. If God would only use His own fingers, and make me broken bread and poured-out wine in a special way! But when He uses someone whom we dislike, or some set of circumstances to which we said we would never submit, we object. We must never choose the scene of our own martyrdom. If ever we are going to be made wine to drink, we will have to be crushed; you cannot drink grapes. Grapes become wine only when they have been squeezed."

Christianity is life with the new dimension— the dimension of eternity. It is life with a goal. That goal is not death but the life that lies on the other side of the grave. Nor is that goal old age, but a new age.

2

THE CHRISTIAN'S IDEAL FOR LIFE
Philippians 2

T HE HIGHEST idealism in all the realm of moral thought is found in the Christian faith and it is specifically expressed in this chapter of the epistle. This Christian idealism is related to the mind and is found in the chapter's key verse 5, "Let this mind be in you, which was also in Christ Jesus."

Jesus Christ is projected as the Christian's ideal for life. As principle must underline practice so the most practical realism must be inspired by the highest idealism; and since thought is the prelude to proper action, it is the mind which must be furnished with the most inspiring ideals. These are found in Jesus Christ.

The idealism of this chapter concerns two things: First, our personal conduct and second, the person of Christ.

I. OUR PERSONAL CONDUCT. Verses 1-4.

"If there be therefore any consolation in Christ, if any comfort of love, if any fellowship of the Spirit, if any bowels and mercies, Fulfil ye my joy, that ye be likeminded, having the same love, being of one accord, of one mind. Let nothing be done through strife or vainglory; but in lowliness of mind let each esteem other better than themselves. Look not every man on his own things, but every man also on the things of others."

Christian conduct is not the Christian version of an old Testament legalism. It is not a matter of rules which detail every deed. It is not an artificial regulation of life. It is first of all a state of mind and this means more than a mental attitude. It means a new mind, a new mental climate, a complete new posture of thought. It means an internal inspiration for living rather than an external regulation by restrictive laws. It is not thought for thought's sake but for life's sake. We are "to think like men of action and act like men of thought." We are not automatons but autonomous. We are free to act but our action can only be free so long as it is in line with the idealism of Jesus Christ.

The essential difference between the Christian's mind and thought life and the world about him is the difference between mental wisdom and moral wisdom. Our school systems are almost solely based on mental wisdom. The structure of our modern mechanical civilization has such a base. Most of the expressed wisdom of modern intellectuals is the "product of an academic system in which the study of moral wisdom has been abandoned" (Walter Lippman). This is the basic weakness of the society of this century. We have collected an amazing amount of technological wisdom but it seriously lacks the moral wisdom found in the Word of God and in the Christian faith. We are building for a fall because we cannot leave morality out of mentality and survive.

The mental attitude of the Christian goes deeper than the usual moral expressions that are current today. It goes back to the mind of Christ. He puts a new value in thinking. He brings a new horizon to the mind. He provides a new standard for thought.

A lawyer came to Jesus upon one occasion and asked Him to name the greatest commandment. Jesus replied that the greatest commandment was to "love the Lord thy God with all thy heart, and with all thy soul, and with all thy mind." Jesus went back to Deuteronomy for this answer to the lawyer but He revised it by substituting mind for strength. Jesus put a new element in our love for God, the mind. To love God with all the heart meant with every warm and tender affection. To love God with all the soul meant with every deep impulse of the new nature. But to love God with "all thy mind" was something new. Men couldn't love God with the mind before Jesus gave it its new direction. Sin had alienated and darkened the mind and it was incapable of thinking God's thoughts after Him. Jesus restored it to its place of responsiveness in the moral structure and made it possible for men to once more love God with all the mind.

We have before us in the text of this epistle the basis for two greatly desired things, Christian unity and Christian conduct.

1. The Basis of Christian Unity. Verses 1, 2.

> "If there be therefore any consolation in Christ, if any comfort of love, if any fellowship of the Spirit, if any bowels and mercies, fulfil ye my joy, that ye be likeminded, having the same love, being of one accord, of one mind."

The rallying point of the appeal for this unity is found in four "ifs" in this passage. "If there be any consolation in Christ," or encouragement in Christ; "if there be any comfort in love," or incentive in love; "if there be any fellowship of the Spirit," or participation in the Spirit; "if there be any bowels and mercies," or affection and sympathy (compassion). If any of these things exist they are the basis of incentive to Christian unity. Paul is not doubtful that these things exist. They are the positive premise of his appeal for a likeminded attitude of common affection and communion among Christians.

Unity is apparently the highest expression of Christian conduct for it is first mentioned. Perhaps because it is first desired, for the best forms of Christian behavior spring from united Christian affection and sympathy.

Unity is more than a doctrinal consideration. It springs from such things as consolation, comfort, fellowship and compassion. Unity seldom comes from our mechanical insistence upon strait doctrinal regularity. It never comes out of the atmosphere of criticism and condemnation. When it is achieved it comes through the expression and exhibition of these factors of fellowship which spring from love and its manifestations. This is so because most men do not react to rational principles. They are emotional creatures and respond to these stimuli.

Christian "likemindedness" consists of three things:

(1) *Of one love.*

Without love knowledge can become divisive instead of cohesive. The giants of the Reformation including Luther, Melanchthon, and Erasmus were men of great intellect and unfaltering courage, who became a group of quarreling and fractious theologians failing in love.

(2) *Of one accord.*

This is a common accord or functioning in unison and harmony and literally means *joint-soul.*

(3) *Of one mind.*

Here is thinking inspired by love and concentrated on a common purpose and action.

It should be remembered that the achievement of this unity of "oneness" of love, of accord and of mind is through the encouragement which comes from Christ, the incentive which is in love, the participation which comes through the Spirit, and through the affection and sympathy which is in our renewed natures.

Such as is mentioned here concerning unity, harmony, co-operation and walking together in love's agreement—all of these are the mark of spiritual maturity. They come with spiritual growth and advancement. One's mature experience will verify the observation that disunity among God's people or in God's work is seldom occasioned except by spiritually immature people. They may have had adult knowledge of doctrine but they were not matured beyond a state of spiritual adolescence.

2. The Basis of Christian Conduct. Verses 3, 4.

> "Let nothing be done through strife or vainglory; but in lowliness of mind let each esteem other better than themselves. Look not every man on his own things, but every man also on the things of others."

Christian unity and Christian conduct are parallel parts of a sound Christian idealism.

The Christian conduct enjoined upon the Philippians was both negative and positive.

(1) *It was negative.* Verses 3, 4.

> "Let nothing be done through strife or vainglory" (verse 3).
> "Look not every man on his own things" (verse 4).

It is impossible to achieve unity in the Christian community if we act in the party spirit; if what we do is in strife; or if it is done in selfishness and conceit. These things engender divisions and cause fragmentation in the people of God.

(2) *It was positive.* Verses 3, 4.

> "In lowliness of mind let each esteem other better than themselves" (verse 3).
> "But every man also on the things of others" (verse 4).

Here is that noble virtue of Christian deference which is the antithesis of the selfishness that causes one to constantly look "on his own things." It is required of each of us if our conduct is to match the idealism of our faith that we "esteem other better than themselves." This is a deferring humility which bids another walk first upon the path of our Christian fellowship. It would spare us much jealousy and save us from much rivalry if ours was the spirit of Christian deference. Too often we look on the things of others with covetousness, envying what they have; or criticism, scorning what they do, rather than with deference and gratitude. We will enjoy our own things more if we will envy others less.

There is the difference in verse 4 of two forces. In physics we learn of centripetal force and centrifugal force. Centripetal force moves inward with everything directed toward the center. Centrifugal

force moves outward with everything directed toward the circumference. When we "look . . . on
our own things" we are living centripetally. When
we "look . . . on the things of others" we are living
centrifugally. One is self-indulging and the other is
self-enlarging. One begins with selfishness and
creates more selfishness with its discontent; the
other begins with self-forgetfulness and creates
good will, happiness, joy and great satisfaction.

Those who make the most conspicuous success
in life are not the ones who seek to possess for the
sake of possessing, but those who seek to serve for
the sake of serving. Serving is primary. Possessing
is secondary. Possessing is the result and reward of
serving. The man who works for a wage is a slave.
The man who works for his work is a master. The
housewife who works simply to achieve a clean
house is a timeserver. The one who works for love
is a queen. There is yet time, no matter what the
years of our life may be, to review and rearrange
life so that its motives are the pure and true ideals
of the Christian faith.

II. THE PERSON OF CHRIST. Verses 5-11.

"Let this mind be in you, which was also in Christ
Jesus: Who, being in the form of God, thought it
not robbery to be equal with God: But made himself of no reputation, and took upon him the form
of a servant, and was made in the likeness of men:
And being found in fashion as a man, he humbled

himself, and became obedient unto death, even the death of the cross. Wherefore God also hath highly exalted him, and given him a name which is above every name: That at the name of Jesus every knee should bow, of things in heaven, and things in earth, and things under the earth; And that every tongue should confess that Jesus Christ is Lord, to the glory of God the Father."

The transmission of the idealism of Christianity is not through creeds or words, but through the person of Jesus Christ. It is by the life of Christ living and expressing itself within us. Hence personal conduct has its source, power and inspiration in the person of Christ. Who He is determines what we can be. It will do us no good to say that it makes little difference who Jesus Christ is for there can be no separation of doctrinal Christianity from practical Christianity.

The delineation of Jesus is found in one of the greatest, most sublime and most profound statements of all the Bible. It is found in the words of verses 5-11.

When in verse 5 it says, "Let this mind be in you, which was also in Christ Jesus," we are not being told to attempt to become little models of Jesus or religious imitations of His character. This could never be. What we are being asked to do is to be motivated and inspired and guided by the same purposes, the same attitudes and the same standards as were in the mind of Christ, for Jesus

Christ is the revelation of God's mind to us. The thrilling possibility of this lies in the fact that through our positional relationship to Christ all the resources of His power are potentially in our possession and can be applied through faith to empower us in our Christian conduct. When we live in a state of spiritual abandonment to Christ, we will be filled with Him and consequently with His desires, purposes and goodness.

Let us see who Christ was:

1. He was Divine—His Pre-Existence. Verse 6.

"Who, being in the form of God, thought it not robbery to be equal with God."

The meaning of this verse turns on the term "in the form of God." Does this mean essence or appearance, real or symbolic, fact or fiction? It is a description of a state antecedent to Christ's historical appearance and tells of His pre-existence, not merely as an appearance but as an actual essence. He was, is and ever shall be God in the sense in which no one of human form was, is or ever can be God. This parallels John's expression: "In the beginning was the Word, and the Word was with God, and the one Word was God" (John 1:1).

What is narrated here is the form of manifestation which characterized Jesus' pre-existence. It is "the former divinely glorious position which He afterwards gave up in His incarnation" (Meyer's Commentary).

To speak of Jesus being in "the form of God" means much more than a godlike capacity. There are many men who are godlike. That cannot be a proper estimate of Christ for He was God and not merely godlike. He was the essence of deity in the appearance of humanity. What He was before incarnation is described in verse 6 as "form." What He looked like after incarnation is described in verse 8 as "fashion." The fashion was not the form but it displayed and revealed God to man sufficient for the purposes of salvation.

Jesus did not become God when He became man. He was God before He was born and He remained God after He became man, but it was in a self-limiting sense so that "the form of God" was veiled in the flesh of man. Jesus had a deity that was pre-human, pre-earthly, pre-Bethlehem, and pre-Mary. He speaks of Himself in these words: "O Father, glorify thou me with thine own self with the glory which I had with thee before the world was" (John 17:5).

2. He was Human—His Incarnation. Verse 7.

> "But made himself of no reputation, and took upon
> him the form of a servant, and was made in the
> likeness of men."

Although He was God in His pre-existent form, He did not selfishly cling to His divine prerogatives. Nor did He graspingly desire to retain this divine equality in all the glory in which He knew it before

Bethlehem. Instead He became willing to surrender and give up the pre-existent glories and accept the humiliation of the incarnation. We call this the *kenosis* or the emptying of Jesus. Of what did this emptying consist? Some kenotic theories assume that Jesus, in this emptying, divested Himself of the possession of His deity so that for the period of His human manifestation He was without the sense, the substance and the power of God. Others declare that Christ had the full divine majesty but only manifested it occasionally. These views are inconsistent with the facts of both Scripture and history.

That of which Jesus did empty or divest Himself was neither His divine powers or prerogatives, but rather the independent use of those powers and prerogatives. Consequently when He was born, He was born of the Holy Spirit; when He spoke, He spoke the words of His Father; when He wrought a miracle, it was not in His own independent power; when He died and when He was raised from the dead, it was all accomplished by Christ's dependence upon His Father. In other words, it was not done as He might have done it through His own independently possessed divine power but by power dependently granted Him by His Father.

In testimony of this condition of "no reputation" Jesus said: "Verily, verily, I say unto you, The Son can do nothing of himself, but what he seeth the Father do: for what things soever he doeth, these also doeth the Son likewise. For the Father loveth the Son, and sheweth him all things that himself doeth: and he will shew him greater works than these, that ye may marvel. For as the Father raiseth up the dead, and quickeneth them; even so the Son quickeneth whom he will. For the Father judgeth no man, but hath committed all judgment unto the Son: that all men should honour the Son, even as they honour the Father. He that honoureth not the Son honoureth not the Father which hath sent him" (John 5:19-23).

Actually making Himself of "no reputation" consisted both of what He gave up and what He took up. What He gave up in the process of incarnation was "the form of God" and this was His pre-human form of existence as a member of the Trinity, including its glories, prerogatives and powers. What He took up in the experience of the incarnation was "the form of a servant" and "the likeness of men." But whatever He gave up and whatever He took up, He remained in nature whatever He was before this giving up and taking up— God. He was truly man but He was more than man. He remained God in all His wisdom, character and power; but He voluntarily surrendered the independent use of those powers, and for redemption's purpose He was made subject in every thought, word and act to the will of God. More than divesting Himself of deity, He invested life with a new and unknown sense of the presence and power of God.

Christ's self-emptying consisted in the following:

He Walked in His Father's Ways—John 16:28
He Willed His Father's Will—John 5:30
He Spoke His Father's Word—John 14:24
He Did His Father's Work—John 17:4
He Rejoiced in His Father's Love—John 10:17
He Sought His Father's Aid—John 11:41
He Aimed at His Father's Glory—John 8:49

3. He Was Obedient—His Atonement. Verse 8.

"And being found in fashion as a man, he humbled himself, and became obedient unto death, even the death of the cross."

The incarnation consisted of putting Jesus in "fashion as a man." Fashion is a mode of dress in which we make our appearance before men. It was similarly true that Jesus' incarnation was the fashion of His appearance to the whole world. Here the word "fashion" means "scheme" and is precisely the same expression that we use for modes of dress. It is used in I Corinthians 7:31 where it speaks of "the fashion of this world" passing away. And the word "world" at this point is the same as it is in II Peter 3 where it is described as dissolving and passing away. The scheme or fashion of this cosmos is its outward dress, social order, customs, costumes, modes and manners of life.

Jesus is presented in history in the fashion and likeness of man and while in that appearance humbles Himself and becomes "obedient." To what is Jesus obedient? It is "unto death." In His incarnation He became obedient unto life and gave up His pre-existent glory. In His crucifixion He became obedient unto death, giving up His pre-existent life.

The crucial fitness of the world's Redeemer was to be in the realm of His obedience because the original fall of man consisted of disobedience. To re-establish, as was His purpose, the relationship of a sovereign God and a disobedient humanity, it could only be done on the basis of obedience in the Redeemer.

This obedience involved a cross, and the death Jesus died on that cross was not an involuntary death in which death overtook Him. He did not die because He had to but because He chose to. As a modern writer puts it, "If the cross were only the story of a man hanging on a beam of wood, giving his life for what he deeply loved, sacrificing his all for what he believed, any good newspaper reporter could tell that story in a few paragraphs. In fact, history is filled with such martyrs and in the passing of most of them humanity did not miss a heartbeat. Crosses are as familiar on the road of history as oak leaves in autumn. What makes the cross of Christ different?"

The difference in the death of Christ upon the cross consists of the fact that Jesus could not have died naturally. He could not have died of sickness, starvation, accident, or even by crucifixion. The only way He could die was by obedience to God and so we read His own description of His death: "Therefore doth my Father love me, because I lay down my life, that I might take it again. No man taketh it from me, but I lay it down of myself. I have power to lay it down, and I have power to take it again. This commandment have I received of my Father" (John 10:17, 18).

Since death was a penalty resulting from sin, then death was something foreign to Jesus who was without sin. Since He was born and lived without sin, He did not need to suffer because of it and He could not succumb to it. Jesus need not have died at all, except He personally and willingly chose to die in obedience to God's will and for our need.

Jesus' death was a biological necessity. He needed to die in order that we might live and only through death could His life become ours. Thus, incarnation and crucifixion are two parts of one purpose. In the one a new life came into the world; in the other this new life is given up to whosoever will possess it.

4. He was Exalted—His Resurrection and Ascension. Verse 9.

> "Wherefore God also hath highly exalted him, and given him a name which is above every name."

The procession of redemptive events led us from Sovereign to Servant and from Servant to Saviour. Now it takes us from Saviour to Sovereign through the resurrection and ascension. In this exaltation Christ resumes the independent exercise of His divine attributes and He is invested with the glories of His pre-existent glory.

Specifically this exaltation is described as God's act of giving Him "a name which is above every name." This actually means *the* name.

When Jesus came into the world in His incarnation, man gave Him a name of humiliation—Jesus —because "He would save His people from their sins." When He went from the world in His ascension God gave Him a name of exaltation. This is a name above every name. It is the name of supreme majesty, supreme glory, supreme power, supreme place and supreme authority. This is the incommunicable name of Jehovah, the Lord, as an appellation of unapproachable dignity and position.

5. He is Supreme—His Return. Verses 10, 11.

> "That at the name of Jesus every knee should bow, of things in heaven, and things in earth, and things under the earth; and that every tongue should confess that Jesus Christ is Lord, to the glory of God the Father."

It will not be at the *name Jesus* but at the *name of Jesus* (Lightfoot) that every knee shall bow and every tongue confess to His Lordship. It will be before the revealed majesty of the exalted and returning Lord that all creation will make obeisance. The supremacy of Jesus Christ will be registered in two significant ways: First, through the adoration of every knee bowing. Second, through the acknowledgment of every tongue confessing. This does not mean a universal restitution of unbelieving men but rather a final and involuntary recognition by all creation of the Lordship of Christ.

When the name of Jesus has been whispered in tender devotion, it has incited adoration and praise. It has been linked with cradle and cross, with healing and life, with ministry and love. When the new name of Jesus' heavenly sovereignty and glory shall be heard, it will leap with radionic power through heaven and earth and it will command immediate respect and unquestioned obedience. Because of it the entire universe, or what is here described as "things in heaven, and things in earth, and things under the earth," will respond in instant obedience. These elements are things and powers visible and invisible, animate, inanimate, and conscious in earth, in heaven and in hell. All these elements will submit to the dominion of His majesty and power.

The result of this will be the restoration of unity to all nature, all earth and heaven. You have perhaps watched a great conductor bringing every member of his orchestra into action toward the close of some mighty music, have seen him, as the music climbed higher and higher, signalling to one player after another, and always at the signal another instrument responding to the summons and adding its voice to the music, until at the last crashing chords not one was left dumb, but all were uniting in a thrilling and triumphant climax. So the Son of God summons everything in creation to swell the glorious unison of God's praise. He signals to the sun riding in the heavens, "You come in now, and praise Him!"—then to the myriad stars of night, "You now, praise Him!"—then to the mountains, raking the clouds with their summits, "Praise Him!" —then to the kings and judges of the earth, "Praise Him!"—then to young manhood in its strength and maidenhood in its grace and beauty, "Praise Him!" —then to the multitude of saints in earth and heaven, "Praise Him!"—until the wide universe is shouting with every voice the praise of God alone. "While I live," cries the psalmist, "will I praise the Lord: I will sing praises unto my God while I have any being" (J. S. Stewart).

The primary message of this passage is to the church—yet it contains a compelling gospel invitation. Men are offered in grace the provisions of redemption. Inherent in this offer is the choice of receiving Christ the Saviour or the alternative of acknowledging Christ the sovereign under the irresistible compulsion of His exaltation. Now we *may* bow and confess: then we *must* bow and acknowledge. Now it is *by choice*: then it will be *by command*. Now it may be *in worship*: then it will be *in obeisance*. Now our tongues may speak *in confession*: then they will speak *in admission*.

III. The Christian's Salvation. Verses 12, 13.

> "Wherefore, my beloved, as ye have always obeyed,
> not as in my presence only, but now much more
> in my absence, work out your own salvation with
> fear and trembling. For it is God which worketh
> in you both to will and to do of his good pleasure."

We must decisively distinguish between Christianity as a divine redemption or a human religion. As a divine redemption it is something we *work out*: but as a human religion it is something we would *work for*. As a divine redemption it is a *cause*: but as a human religion it would be an *effect*. As a divine redemption it is the *gift of God's grace*: but as a human religion it would be the *result of human effort*.

We must revert here, for perspective's sake, to the original concept of this epistle that Christianity is a life. It is Christ's life implanted within the human spirit. This implanted life is to be expressed through our lives so that we may say "for to me to live is Christ." In this concept it is an effect rather than an effort. It is a devotion rather than a duty. It is not localized to buildings or confined to one day. It is not a problem to be solved by inquiry but a power to be applied through identification with Christ.

The Christian's salvation appears in these words of the text: "Wherefore, my beloved, as ye have always obeyed, not as in my presence only,

but now much more in my absence, work out your
own salvation with fear and trembling. For it is
God which worketh in you both to will and to do
of his good pleasure." The introducing word here
is "wherefore" and it links the obedience of the
Christian believer to the obedience of our Lord.
In verse 8 we see Christ obedient unto death in
the provision of salvation. In verse 12 we see the
Christian obedient unto life in the experience of
salvation. Obedience to the will of God is essential
both in salvation's provision and its proving.

Upon a partial and cursory reading of our
present passage, salvation is concluded by some
readers to be a work of human achievement and
effort rather than divine grace. This it cannot be
for it would then throw it out of consonance with
the rest of Scripture.

There are two meanings in this much misun-
derstood passage: The first meaning is as a warning
against the danger of being proxy Christians. There
appears to have been a tendency upon the part of
some of the Philippians to be Christians by proxy.
Paul says to them, "Wherefore . . . as ye have always obeyed, not as in my presence only, but now
much more in my absence, work out your own
salvation." They apparently tended to lean upon
Paul and depend on his presence for strength. They
were strong and bold in his presence but weak and
fearful in his absence. It was necessary that they
thoroughly develop themselves in Christian exper-

ience and mature their faith so they could stand on their own feet. Hence the injunction, "Work out your own salvation."

This is being Christian by proxy, through the devotion and strength of another. It is what happens when husbands demur and say in effect, Let my wife be Christian for me. Or when church members say in effect, Let the pastor be Christian for me. It is enough that he do the praying, the reading of God's Word and the witnessing. I will pay toward his support and he can be my proxy. Or when some Christian says in effect, Let God be Christian for me. It is enough that I am saved, now let God do the rest; and in consequence of this attitude he neither *works at* or *works out* his Christian life. This proxy attitude will be fatal to the best interests of any person for he will remain in the adolescence of spiritual immaturity and lose the joy of an advancing life in Christ.

The second meaning of this passage is that there is an out-worked labor upon our part on the basis of an in-worked life on God's part.

1. The Out-Worked Labor. Verse 12.

> "Wherefore, my beloved, as ye have always obeyed, not as in my presence only, but now much more in my absence, work out your own salvation with fear and trembling."

To be sure it says that we are to "work out our own salvation" but it also goes on to say "it is God which worketh in you." Salvation is something to be worked out, not in order to be saved, but because we are already saved.

There are two words for "work" in these verses. In verse 13 the word "worketh in you" refers to God's work, while in verse 12 the word "work out" refers to man's work. But they are not the same words and consequently do not have the same meaning. The word for work in verse 13 is the word from which we get our word "energy," and it refers to God's work of divine power in us at the time of regeneration. This energy of power will be the reason and cause for our ability to work out our salvation as an experience. The word for "work" in verse 12 means to "thoroughly develop" in the sense of completing and maturing what has been commenced. And when applied to the first word "work" it means to thoroughly develop the nature which God has implanted by divine energy.

This means that there are two aspects to the experience of salvation—the divine and the human. In the divine aspect salvation is initiated and provided through the historical work of redemption. In the human aspect salvation is appropriated and developed in the experience of the Christian. None of us can create the divine energy which is worked in us; but each of us must allow this implanted life to thoroughly develop in and through us. Just as the flower has received the energy of flower-life and permits that energy to work itself out in the form, beauty and perfume of the flower, so we are to allow the energy of the Christ-life to be worked out in us.

Apart from the extremes of dogmatic theological concepts we must understand both the human and divine aspects of salvation. The human side is to work out what God has worked in. It, therefore, requires the conscious effort of the child of God in using the means of grace which God has provided. And in this concept contemplation and worship are not just adoration, but an inspiration for action. Bible reading is not just meditation, but the prelude of doing. Prayer is not just expression; it is preparation for duty. Once a mother heard her son praying. She noticed that what he was doing was to tell God what he planned to do and seeking to direct God to help him. The mother said to her son, "Son, don't bother to give God instructions, just report for duty." Thus salvation and Christian experience are the balanced combination of divine energy plus human action with its work, adventure, responsibility and achievement.

Salvation is both an act and a process. The act of saving us is by God's gift. The process of being saved is by God's grace. The act is justification. The process is sanctification. The act of God results in the gift of a new life. The process of grace develops and matures that new life.

When we work out our salvation we are not trying to *work for* that salvation. Salvation is not something you earn either partially or entirely.

Salvation is solely and completely an act of sovereign grace apart from human merit or effort.

When God works in the new life that is our *standing before God.* When we work out this new life that is our *state before men.* One results in an eternal position which cannot change and the other results in an earthly condition which does change as we develop and grow in grace. It may even fluctuate forward and backward.

We are not to think of this as co-operating with God in the sense that God needs our help to save us. Salvation is not a religious agreement or bargain with God in which man promises to be good in exchange for divine favor. What co-operation is involved begins after, not before, salvation becomes a fact. Death cannot co-operate with life. Ignorance cannot co-operate with knowledge. Sinfulness cannot co-operate with righteousness. Nor can the sinner, dead in trespasses and sins, co-operate with God in the saving act. The beginning of all Christian experience is the inworked energy of a divine life. The end and aim of all Christian experience is the outworked effect of this divine life.

We cannot work out what God has not worked in. This is no more true in man than in nature. There are vast resources of natural wealth in the minerals that lie within the earth which are being taken out at the rate of billions of dollars every year. But no miner can work out gold or diamonds or copper from the earth which the Creator did not work in. The same is true of electricity. We harness our motors to its mighty power but that power would not be there unless God allowed it.

One of the most remarkable characters of our day was the late George Washington Carver who was born a slave and once was traded for a horse. "Years ago, before the slaves were free, a little six-months-old Negro boy was stolen, with other slaves, from his owner, Moses Carver, who lived near Diamond Grove, Missouri. Carver sent some men to get his slaves back. They struck a bargain for the baby, traded an old horse for him, and brought him back.

"That baby became a professor in Tuskegee University. He held the degrees of bachelor and master and honorary doctor of science, and he was a member of the Royal Society for the Encouragement of Arts, Manufactures and Commerce of Great Britain. He was a musician, and once toured the Middle West as a concert pianist. He was a painter, and had exhibited at the great world's fairs.

"But the most surprising thing about him was his ability to make things out of nothing—paint out of clay, marble out of wood shavings, starch, paste, vinegar, ink, shoe blacking, molasses and caramels out of sweet potatoes. Listen now and see whether you think you could do it: he has made butter, oil, cheese, dye-stuff, face powder, breakfast food, printer's ink, pickles, instantaneous coffee, axle grease, and two hundred and seventy-six other things—out of peanuts.

"Now maybe you have to be a Negro boy born in a slave cabin and stolen from your owner and traded for a horse before you can do such things. But I wouldn't let that thought stop me. I'd try to keep my eyes open to see whether there isn't something in ordinary things that ordinary people don't see there. For, as Professor Carver himself said, 'When you do common things in an uncommon way, you will command the attention of the world.'"

George Washington Carver was classified as a genius but he did not profess to be one. He attributed all his success to the recognition of God. He said that whatever he did he was doing it because God had already placed the possibility of it in nature. He was doing what God told him to do. He was doing, in the physical realm, what we might do in the spiritual realm if we recognized what he did.

We must hold in view the important fact that the practical lies alongside the spiritual. In the canon of Scripture it has been pointed out (Prof. J. Ritchie Smith) that Psalms and Proverbs lie side by side. They lie side by side in life, too. The order of Scripture is the order of experience. First, religion is enshrined in the heart — that is the Psalms. Second, religion is worked out in the life — that is Proverbs. Religion can put on her beautiful garments and move into the temple to worship on Sunday. But she must then go home and put on her everyday clothes and go to work in the workshops of life. The religion that is found at the altar on Sunday should be found at the sink and the counter on Monday. If you know certain things are true on Sunday, do them on Monday. You've got to be someone's New Testament the rest of the week. It is the New Testament in book covers on Sunday. It is to be the same New Testament in shoe leather on Monday.

It says in this verse 12 that this salvation is to be worked out "with fear and trembling." To what extent is our Christianity a fearful and trembling effort? This has no reference to the tormenting misgivings which some have associated with salvation which they assume to be a precarious religious possession they must keep at the expense of fear and apprehension. It means, rather, the spirit of reverence and trust with which we should enter upon and live our Christian lives. It is not with fear and dread but with reverence to God in the living of life and consequently joy and peace in the experience of living.

In the Christian concept of life God is the companion of the believer and the indweller of the human personality. Consequently with God at the center of experience, our life is not to be identified either with pagan or modern environmental corruption. It is to be in Christian separation in which we, with our reverence for God, have an equal reverence for life and refuse to identify God with iniquity and evil. This is to be the measure of our "fear and trembling."

2. The In-Worked Life. Verse 13.

> "For it is God which worketh in you both to will
> and to do of his good pleasure."

The genius of the Christian life lies in the in-worked energy or power of God with which He wills and does of His good pleasure.

We recognize the inward presence of God in the contracted verse which then says "God . . . in you." In the Revised Standard Version the phrase "it is God which worketh in you" is translated "for God is at work in you." Here are words to thrill the soul. God is not only in us as a holy companion but God is at work in us. He is the God of the galaxies, the Lord of the constellations, the continents and seas, the God of the centuries and ages. This God is at work in the Christian, His latest creation, His newest and greatest product. The pattern to which He is working is His Son—"For whom he did foreknow, he also did predestinate to be conformed to the image of his Son" (Rom. 8:29).

A few years ago Albert Einstein took up residence in Pasadena, California, in a modest and unpretentious house not far from the California Institute of Technology. Immediately that house became the object of great interest. People drove past it in their cars. They walked by it. They stood outside of it. Why? What was the reason? Albert Einstein was at work in that house. But of greater interest is the fact that God is at work in the Christian. What holy attention and calculated wonder that should command!

While they were building the great six million dollar Freeway Bridge across the Arroyo Seco in Pasadena, they had a special observation building for the convenience of sidewalk superintendents. A complete scale model of the new structure was there before the visitor, while the giant span itself was in view in its construction form through spacious windows. It is a beautiful structure of steel and concrete and its immensity stirs the admiration of all who have seen it. But a greater and more lasting work is going on in the Christian. When Einstein is forgotten and the Arroyo Seco Bridge is a crumbled ruin, the Christian will be the on-going replica of the work of the Eternal God. In the face of this the attitude should be reverent and submissive respect, for God is at work in us.

God's presence in us is not a mere religious symbol of divine life: it is a working presence and an active force which provides the unlimited resources of this new and divine life of the Christian. It is "according to the power that worketh in us" (Eph. 3:20).

During the construction of one of the East River bridges in New York City the engineers, in sinking their caissons in the river, encountered the sunken hulk of an old barge which would not yield to removal. It had become so securely embedded in the river mud that engines, cables and derricks were powerless to remove it. At this point in the fruitless operation a young man, fresh from technical school, appeared on the scene and after studying the problem asked for permission to try his hand. Upon permission he had a large barge towed to the spot at the approach of low tide and its ends were fastened by huge chains to the sunken hulk. Then when the tide came in with its irresistible power the surface barge rose with the swelling tide, lifting with it the submerged wreck. That young engineer had made use of the limitless natural power of the ocean tides: an example to us that God-linked lives can be lifted and transformed, energized and empowered by the "power that worketh in us."

The purpose of this work of God in us is "to will and to do of His [God's] good pleasure." God is working to accomplish His sovereign will, a prehistoric and pre-redemptive plan conceived in the councils of eternity. In Ephesians 2:10 are the words, "For we are his workmanship, created in Christ Jesus." This word "workmanship" is the same word from which we get our English word "poem." This God who is at work in us is the great eternal poet and our lives are the poems which He is making and which someday will be gathered into a great poem of praise to the glory of the Divine Poet.

IV. THE CHRISTIAN'S LIFE. Verses 14-16.

"Do all things without murmurings and disputings:
that ye may be blameless and harmless, the sons of
God, without rebuke, in the midst of a crooked
and perverse nation, among whom ye shine as
lights in the world; holding forth the word of life;
that I may rejoice in the day of Christ, that I have
not run in vain, neither laboured in vain."

The sequel to salvation is life because salvation
is life. In this case the working out of the in-worked
life is in the practical aspects of daily experience
and this finds its expression in our words, our manners and our public relations.

Ours is the peril of a paradox. Having a great
God we are in danger of being small people who live
small and inconsequential lives. We are in danger
of dissipating energies on insignificant things like
quarreling, faultfinding and disputing. We are in
danger of forgetting that God is at work in us while
we spend ourselves in foolish debate and senseless
controversy. This is surely what Paul means when
he says, "Do all things without murmurings and
disputings." God's purpose for our lives is something better and greater. It is "that ye may be
blameless and harmless, the sons of God, without
rebuke, in the midst of a crooked and perverse
nation, among whom ye shine as lights in the
world."

The environment of the contemporary Philippian society is described as "crooked and perverse."
It was a morally warped and spiritually perverted

society. It is in such environment that every generation of Christians has been placed—morally warped
and spiritually perverted. The degree of the warp
and the extent of the perversion has fluctuated,
to be sure, but the essential nature remains un-
changed because the general character of society
is always a reflection of the character of the individual in that society.

The Christian is placed "in the midst" of such
environments. He is not to live in isolation from
society. He is expected to change it and not to be
changed by it. He is expected to transform it and
not to conform to it. What a tragedy when Christ-
tians, called to such a world-changing ministry as
this, descend to petty and carnal quarreling. Instead of being men they are children quibbling
about the little things, pouting and sulking over
imaginary slights and hurts. May God shame us
out of our petty living to large and useful lives.

Our place in contemporary society is twofold:
1. As an Illuminating Influence. Verse 15.

" . . . among whom ye shine as lights."

Our influence is to be the influence of light.
It is the character of Christians to be light, for
Jesus said of us, "Ye are the light of the world."
We are the light-bearers of our generation and our
shining is to be like the stars of the heavens, shining
against the dark sky of surrounding sin.

The influence of light is a silent but effective

thing. It is much like the influence of inductive electricity. If an electrified wire is brought near an unelectrified wire, the wire containing the current of electricity will cause the other wire to receive a charge of power. Electric impulses in code can be transmitted by induction from one wire to a parallel one. It is possible in this way to telegraph or telephone from moving trains. "There is something like this in our influence upon other souls. There are induced currents for good or bad. You, as a child of God, cannot come in contact with other men who belong to this crooked and perverse generation, without starting within them the vibrations of your own holiness, the yearning for something better than they are, the appetite, the hunger and thirst, after the unseen and the eternal, the condemnation of their sin, and the creation within them of the vibrations and waves of desire to be other than they are. It is also true that you cannot come in contact with a bad man, whose mind is steeped in vice, and whose life is full of base and disgraceful actions, without a corresponding current being induced in yourself. We are always, for good or bad, affecting those who are in close contact with us, and this altogether apart from our volition, and simply by the strength of our character" (F. B. Meyer).

2. As an Active Witness. Verse 16.

"Holding forth the word of life; that I may rejoice

in the day of Christ, that I have not run in vain, neither laboured in vain."

Shining as lights is being a passive Christian influence. Holding forth the word of life is being an active Christian witness. In one case it is being a character witness. In the other case it is being an articulate witness. You cannot hold forth the word of life without words. In one case it is vocational. In the other case it is vocal. In one case it is by life. In the other case it is by lip. In one case it is illumination. In the other case it is proclamation. We are to be both lights and voices, to shine and to speak, to be felt and to be heard.

The purpose for shining and witnessing was the extension of Jesus Christ into human affairs by regeneration. This regeneration is to be by spiritual generation and this generation of life is through the influence of the Christian witness. It is of the nature of everything that lives from the lowly cell to exalted man to pass on its nature in another life, to multiply itself, to exist for the sake of reproduction. Spiritual reproduction is the responsibility of every child of God. The vehicle of this spiritual reproduction is the Word of God.

Paul was concerned for the Philippian Christians lest his efforts die with them; lest they absorb the benefits and blessings of the Christian life without passing them on to contemporaries. So he says, "that I may rejoice in the day of Christ, that I have not run in vain, neither laboured in vain." There is to be a cumulative effect in Christian service. It goes on from generation to generation. It extends from one to another. It multiplies through bright shining and faithful voicing.

The language Paul uses at this point is sharpened by Way's translation: "that I have not run my race for a phantom prize, nor toiled for an elusive way." Think of the many who are running for phantom prizes, prizes that never materialize; and are working for elusive wages, wages that are never paid. Life is full of illusion and frustration and multitudes are striving to achieve goals they will never reach.

On the ceiling of the great State Hall in the Palace at Versailles is a painting of Hercules in appropriate mythological surroundings. It took the artist two and one-half years of continuous labor to complete this magnificent work. When he received no pay for it, he committed suicide in that very room and beneath his great painting. Life seemed without purpose to him in the absence of a commensurate reward. But there is a true sense in which the fruit of our labor, whether recognized or not, is reward enough. However, God will be faithful to us and when one invests his life as an influence and witness, he will have his certain reward.

V. THE CHRISTIAN'S EXAMPLE. Verses 17-30.

"Yea, and if I be offered upon the sacrifice and service of your faith, I joy, and rejoice with you all.

For the same cause also do ye joy, and rejoice with me. But I trust in the Lord Jesus to send Timotheus shortly unto you, that I also may be of good comfort, when I know your state. For I have no man likeminded, who will naturally care for your state. For all seek their own, not the things which are Jesus Christ's. But ye know the proof of him, that, as a son with the father, he hath served with me in the gospel. Him therefore I hope to send presently, so soon as I shall see how it will go with me. But I trust in the Lord that I also myself shall come shortly. Yet I supposed it necessary to send to you Epaphroditus, my brother, and companion in labour, and fellowsoldier, but your messenger, and he that ministered to my wants. For he longed after you all, and was full of heaviness, because that ye had heard that he had been sick. For indeed he was sick nigh unto death: but God had mercy on him; and not on him only, but on me also, lest I should have sorrow upon sorrow. I sent him therefore the more carefully, that, when ye see him again, ye may rejoice, and that I may be the less sorrowful. Receive him therefore in the Lord with all gladness; and hold such in reputation: Because for the work of Christ he was nigh unto death, not regarding his life, to supply your lack of service toward me."

Supporting the idealism which is found in this chapter are the examples of three outstanding proponents of the Christian faith, Paul, Timothy and Epaphroditus. If one picture is worth a thousand words one life shining and vocal is worth a multitude of theories and creeds.

1. Paul. Verses 17,18.

> "Yea, and if I be offered upon the sacrifice and service of your faith, I joy, and rejoice with you all. For the same cause also do ye joy, and rejoice with me."

Paul was a living example of practical, demonstrable, effective Christianity. He speaks of himself as "a libation upon the sacrificial offering of your faith" (Revised Standard Version). He is willing that his life be a constant sacrifice for the achievement of the aims and goals of the Christian life.

Sacrifice and not self-indulgence is the basis of all achievement and it is specifically true in the spiritual life. The self-sacrificing life, like a poured out libation or offering, is the great contributor to the world's blessing and betterment. This is not an accidental achievement. It is on purpose.

2. Timothy. Verses 19-23.

> "But I trust in the Lord Jesus to send Timotheus shortly unto you, that I also may be of good comfort, when I know your state. For I have no man likeminded, who will naturally care for your state. For all seek their own, not the things which are Jesus Christ's. But ye know the proof of him, that, as a son with the father, he hath served with me in the gospel. Him therefore I hope to send presently, so soon as I shall see how it will go with me."

You gather from this passage the great importance of Timothy to Paul. He was likeminded or
"equal souled" with an affinity of mind and spirit
that united him to Paul in faithful comradeship and
unselfish service. While others sought their own
interest, their own ease and comfort, and went
about to establish their own reputation, Timothy
was concerned with "the things which are Jesus
Christ's."

Timothy's devotion was in spite of a physical
handicap. He was "delicately reared" and possessed a weak constitution. He undoubtedly suffered from a congenital condition which kept him
from being rugged and robust. But in spite of this
physical handicap, he was the one among all Paul's
companions who was most dependable and useful.

No doubt each of us can recall to his shame
the small measure of his devotion to Christ. How
seldom have we been willing to surrender our ease
for His cause. How often we have defended our
reputation and lost His blessing. How quick we
have been to nourish our own affections and support our own interests and lost the larger things
of Christ.

Timothy's life is an example which proves that
physical circumstances are not immediately necessary to our happiness. He overrode the disability
of a weak body and the lack of a rugged constitution. He ministered out of his weakness in those
things which made other people strong. He con-

tributed out of the realm of the spirit those qualities that cause the weak things to conquer the
strong. No matter who we are and where we are,
we have in Christ the things that can change any
life situation.

3. Epaphroditus. Verses 24-30.

"But I trust in the Lord that I also myself shall come
shortly. Yet I supposed it necessary to send to you
Epaphroditus, my brother, and companion in
labour, and fellowsoldier, but your messenger, and
he that ministered to my wants. For he longed after
you all, and was full of heaviness, because that ye
had heard that he had been sick. For indeed he
was sick nigh unto death: but God had mercy on
him; and not on him only, but on me also, lest I
should have sorrow upon sorrow. I sent him therefore the more carefully, that, when ye see him
again, ye may rejoice, and that I may be the less
sorrowful. Receive him therefore in the Lord with
all gladness; and hold such in reputation: Because
for the work of Christ he was nigh unto death,
not regarding his life, to supply your lack of service
toward me."

Epaphroditus was a messenger of mercy sent
by the Philippian church to succor Paul in his need
at Rome. He was now about to return to Philippi
bearing this epistle. While at Rome Epaphroditus
was taken desperately ill and his life was despaired
of. His illness affords us an example of what all
Christians must inevitably face in the experiences
of life. Can we learn from Epaphroditus that God

will miraculously heal all manner of sickness in answer to prayer?

The only clue we have to the almost fatal sickness of this servant of God is in verse 30: "Because for the work of Christ he was nigh unto death, not regarding his life, to supply your lack of service toward me." His sickness was not a divine punishment for deliberate sin, or the natural consequence of broken law. It was the cumulative result of a long and hazardous journey to reach Rome by land and sea. Out of physical exhaustion and weakness he fell prey to some form of a dangerous disease which almost proved fatal.

There are very few cases of actual sickness mentioned in the New Testament when we get past the Book of Acts. Among these few are Epaphroditus, Timothy, Trophimus and Paul. In none of these cases is sickness the result of sin. In Paul's case it was "a messenger of Satan." In Timothy's case it was due to a natural physical sensitiveness. In Epaphroditus it was the result of overexertion from travel.

Epaphroditus' recovery is described very simply: "but God had mercy on him" (verse 27). Here was a definite act of divine healing in which God interposed His mercy for His sick servant. The intervention was real and crucial for he was "sick nigh unto death," but God produced curative powers that brought this needed servant back to healthful vigor.

It is to be noted that God did not do this in every case of sickness to which we have referred. It was not always by providential intervention. In Paul's case He did not heal but gave grace to bear the physical infirmity. In Timothy's case He did not intervene but the young man was advised to use means for his delicate condition. In the case of Trophimus he was not healed but had to remain at Miletum sick and recover naturally.

We must and do believe that an Almighty God is able and willing in cases of His sovereign choosing to intervene and heal the sick. But a sovereign God also chooses to use physical disability for discipline and gives grace to bear it. In other cases a sovereign God considers that the use of means is wise and legitimate since all these are from His creative hand. It is not for our good or God's glory, nor according to an all-wise God's purpose that life shall be free from the inconveniences of sickness. These can be the instruments of His blessing.

Epaphroditus lingers with us, not like Timothy as a sweet scent of flowers, but like a spiritual stalwart. He was the heroic comrade of Paul who was willing to disregard his own safety and will and hazard all for His Lord. He heads a list of noble souls who follow in his train and through succeeding ages have been advancing the cause of Christ regardless of personal sacrifice and cost.

Epaphroditus also reminds us that tragedy and misfortune live on the same street with health and happiness. "Sooner or later everybody needs a faith or a philosophy of life big enough and strong enough to stand up to disaster. Blessed is he who has his anchor secure before the storm breaks. When what we call disaster breaks upon us, we are too stunned to be able to arrange our ideas, too bewildered to begin to erect our faith" (Leslie D. Weatherhead).

It is never too early to discover how to come to terms with life, so that when the inevitable blow falls we are, at least, partially prepared for it. We can well take a lesson from the dying Scot. In his last moments his daughter asked him if she should read to him from the Bible. "Na, na, lassie," he said, "I theekit (thatched) me hoose in calm weather."

Stretched on the ground in a portion of the redwood forest near Crescent City in California lies a redwood tree called "The Fallen Monarch." Many hundreds of years ago, perhaps several thousand, it was a proud king among the giants of the forest. Probably weakened by previous fire, it was brought crashing to the earth in a storm. Lying there for years it became covered with moss and fern. While apparently conquered by its environmental elements and soon to be swallowed up by its surroundings, the tree did not give up to its fate. From its inward life it pushed out a shoot of new tree life into the light. Year after year it grew from shoot to sapling and then a great towering tree took its place among the giants of that forest. This is characteristic of the redwood of California forests. Undaunted by enemies that bring extinction to other trees these redwoods continue to live and thrive. They are in turn characteristic of God's people and the Christian faith. Throughout the ages God's people have been faced with many calamities, many overwhelming forces, but they illustrate the words of the Prophet Isaiah, "as the days of a tree are the days of my people." It is true nationally of Israel, spiritually of the Church and individually of the Christian.

Roman emperors sought to exterminate the followers of Jesus Christ. After beheading and burning thousands and throwing others to the beasts, they sat back upon their golden chairs with apparent conviction that the Church would disappear. Yet, rooted in divine life, the stricken Church sent forth tendrils of new life and proved once more, "as the days of a tree are the days of my people." Powerful forces abound today which seek to exterminate Christianity. Yet the persistent life of Christ in the Church refuses to die and the Church survives to go on. For every seemingly insurmountable difficulty there is a way to victory, conquest and survival.

3

THE CHRISTIAN'S OBJECT IN LIFE
Philippians 3

IF JESUS CHRIST is the source of life for the Christian and his perfect ideal, it is to be expected that the Christian's objective, desires, hopes, aspirations and attainments will also be found in Him. It is expressed in these words: "What things were gain to me, those I counted loss for Christ" (vs. 7). This chapter tells of four things the apostle desires more than anything else. It is *to win Christ* (vs. 8); *to be found in Christ* (vs. 9); *to know Christ* (vs. 10); *to be like Christ* (vs. 21).

Jesus Christ is the subject of the believer's faith and the object of the believer's life. He defines our creeds and inspires our deeds.

There are seven phases of this life in this chapter:

I. THE CHRISTIAN'S REJOICING. Verse 1.

> "Finally, my brethren, rejoice in the Lord. To write the same things to you, to me indeed is not grievous, but for you it is safe."

The ability to make life a happy and joyful experience is so important and so possible that

Christians ought to employ every means of grace to discover its secret. Paul immediately suggests that the secret of a happy and joyful Christian experience is to "rejoice in the Lord." Apparently he had been urging the Philippians to do this before, even as he does later (4:4). He intimates by his language that, as Christians, they have right to a happy life and consequently he does not consider it irksome to bring this to their attention because it will save them from discouragement by distracting influence in life as well as from the evil influence of false teachers.

Let all Christians rejoice. Let them be happy, contended and inwardly tranquil because the source and center of their life is "in the Lord." This is what it means to "rejoice in the Lord." If we are consciously living in Christ, we have an inward strength which furnishes us with an abiding peace and happiness. When David was in difficulty he "encouraged himself in the Lord." When Israel was in trouble Nehemiah reminded them that "the joy of the Lord is your strength." The late Bishop Taylor Smith suggests that we "aim at making life one unbroken thanksgiving."

There is a certain preserving power in a joyful Christian experience which is unequaled by anything else. It is infectious. It tones up life. It establishes spiritual morale which is so important to our lives. Proverbs says "a merry heart doeth good like a medicine."

Rejoicing is sound spiritual strategy because it is recognition of the profound effect which emotions can have upon our well-being. There are destructive emotions and there are healing emotions which contribute in one case to illness and in the other case to health. One results in unhappiness and the other in happiness. One contributes to instability and the other to stability.

The destructive emotions are not in themselves destructive for they are useful. It is when they get out of control that they are definitely harmful. They are the emotions of *fear* such as anxiety, worry and apprehension; of *anger* such as hostility, resentment, envy, jealousy and hatred; of *guilt feelings* such as the sense of failure, discouragement and depression. All of these have a destructive effect upon us, sometimes affecting glandular secretions but always destroying and tearing down the inner man.

The healing emotions are faith, hope, love and happiness. When these govern our lives they make us strong and consistent and act like a tonic which tones up the whole physical, mental and spiritual system.

The reasons for happiness are lifted from the material and physical level to the spiritual. They are in consequence removed from the fluctuations of changing fortunes and circumstances to the one unchanging element in life—"the Lord."

A few years ago there was an epidemic of suicides in New York City. Upon case investigations of these tragedies, it was remarked by the investigator that these people had everything to live with but nothing to live for.

How can one rejoice in the Lord? Is this a religious cliche? Is this a glib phrase which we throw into meaningless circulation or is it a realizable experience? Is it true particularly when we observe its further emphasis in this epistle (4:4) where Paul says, "Rejoice in the Lord alway"? There is a divine law which governs happiness just as there are divine laws which govern our physical existence and our universe.

Stable and consistent Christian happiness is not made up of shallow emotional exuberance that comes with a whim and goes with a laugh. It is something built upon the solid ground of the laws of our spiritual life. In this there are three rules to follow: (1) *Faith, the Rule of the Heart.* Faith links us with God. One cannot rejoice in the Lord unless and until he is united to the Lord. One cannot rejoice in a deity living in the skies as an impersonal god of space. He must have proximity to us and faith brings God out of heaven and down to earth. God was pleased in the creation to order the soul of man so that it had a natural tendency toward Him and a natural affinity with Him. That soul, however, became disordered by sin and as long as this sinful disorder as a state of character exists, rejoicing will only be an external and artificial thing. It is faith which brings the soul into harmony with God and puts the faculties of that soul in a place to rejoice in God. (2) *Knowledge, the Rule of the Head.* Rejoicing and happiness must be intelligent and based upon knowledge. In this case it is the knowledge of Scripture. If any expect to rejoice in the Lord they must know the Lord in context. *i.e.,* in Scripture. (3) *Cultivation, the Rule of the Will.* He will be happy who wills to be happy. He will be happy who does something about his unhappiness. Jesus said, "Resist the devil, and he will flee from you" and this meant all the devil's brew and brood of destructive emotions. Jesus further said, "If ye know these things, happy are ye if ye do them."

One cultivates happiness by "steadfastly resisting any tendency to murmur or complain; to find fault with God's dealings; or to seek to elicit sympathy. We must resist the temptations to depression and melancholy as we would resist any form of sin. We must insist on watching the one patch of blue in the day sky. Be sure that presently it will overspread the heavens. We must rest upon the promises of God in certain faith that He will triumph gloriously, and that the future will absolutely vindicate the long story of human pain. We must cultivate a cheery optimism and an undaunted hope. We must resolve to imitate Him in whom the poet says, that he—

'Never turned his back, but marched breast
forward,
Never doubted clouds would break,
Never dreamed, though right were worsted,
wrong would triumph,
Hence we fall to rise, are baffled to fight better,
sleep to wake!' "   (F. B. Meyer)

Joy is like virtue: it is kept or lost not by external conditions but by an inner standard of life. It is the result of what is inside rather than of what happens on the outside. Do not try to keep happiness. It cannot be kept any more than you can keep healthy. Keep the laws which govern health and you will enjoy good health; break those laws and they will break you.

Too much of our Christian experience is made up of words and phrases. It is only a dialect of the churches with which we become familiar on Sunday and forget on Monday. There can be no abiding reality in such religion. Christ is only a name when He should be an experience.

Piety often results in a long face when the true contour of our facial Christianity is broad. We speak of broad-minded people when we ought to speak of broad-faced people. Too much of the wrong kind of piety puts wrinkles in the wrong places. In keeping with this Psalm 34:5 speaks: "They looked unto him, and were radiant." This facial radiance is the normal spiritual effect of spiritual proximity to Christ.

A friend of Ralph Waldo Emerson said of him on one occasion that "he came into our house this morning with a sunbeam in his face." This fulfilled Romans 12:8 where Arthur S. Way translates the passage: "If you come with sympathy to sorrow bring God's sunlight in your face."

Dr. Henry Clay Trumbull speaks of a boyhood experience with Adoniram Judson. "One evening he saw a stranger arrive by train in his native town, whose appearance greatly attracted him. He had never seen such a light on a human face before, and at last it dawned upon him that the man was the great missionary, with whose picture he was familiar. He hurried to summon his own minister, and the little lad was soon forgotten as the two fell into deep conversation; but the boy circled about them steadfastly looking on that face. Until the day he died he was accustomed to speak of its beautiful light that shone like the sun."

We usually get the kind of faces we deserve. One thing is sure, we get the face our heart gives us. As a hospital nurse entered her patient's room he said, "She came into the room with her *affidavit* face." Affidavits testify to the validity of a statement and in the case of Christians faces identify and validate characters. It has been said that the face is the map of the mind, the table of contents of the heart, the playground of the emotions, the battlefield of passions, and the landscape of the soul. What do our faces reveal? What would you have your face express?

II. THE CHRISTIAN'S PRESERVATION. Verses 2,3.

> "Beware of dogs, beware of evil workers, beware of the concision. For we are the circumcision, which worship God in the spirit, and rejoice in Christ Jesus, and have no confidence in the flesh."

Looking out of the window of his prison in Rome, Paul probably looked across the huge piles of buildings that were Rome, toward the River Tiber and thence by imagination to Philippi and its meager company of Christians. For them he held a deep concern lest they fall prey to predatory men both religious and pagan.

You have the following here:

1. A Warning Against False Christianity. Verse 2.

> "Beware of dogs, beware of evil workers, beware of the concision."

(1) *"Beware of dogs."*

This was a term of reproach both among the Jews and the Greeks, for dogs in those days were "herds of half-wild animals prowling through the streets, each pack holding its own street against all comers, having neither homes nor masters and feeding on the refuse of the streets, quarreling among themselves and attacking passersby."

Dogs then were not the cultured canines of this twentieth century with manicured and painted toenails, Parisian coiffures, gold-plated collars, hair rinses, shampooes, special predigested food, refrigerated dinners or taxi service to and from canine beauty parlors. Then when their life of hardship is over the canine embalmer, special slumber rooms where their mistresses may come to mourn their passing. And, finally, jacquered caskets with satin pillows for their tired heads, a memorial service to eulogize their canine virtues; and then the long, tearful, sorrowful, agonizing ride to crematory or grave. Ah, no! None of that in Philippi. Instead it was a breed of predatory animals to shun as an object lesson against dangerous humans.

This warning was a well-understood caution against "the prowling mongrels of the Judaizing party" for Epaphroditus had brought Paul news of the presence of these disturbers in Philippi where they had come to ravage God's flock. These Judaizers, and their kind, exist today in numerous sectarian forms. They insisted that Jesus Christ could only be reached through observance of the ceremonial law and that a believer "must be at least something of a Jew to be anything of a Christian."

The Judaizers were not essentially deniers of the faith. They added to it. It was not what they took away so much as what they added, which made their teaching dangerous. They did not deny that faith was the true element in salvation but they added legalism to faith as a requisite of salvation.

You can often make deadly poisons out of harmless chemicals by a simple addition. A few years ago Franklin D. Roosevelt, Jr., was taken ill with a streptococcus infection of the throat. A new remedy called sulphanilamide was tried with amazing success. The publicity of the case caused the drug to be in great demand. A pharmaceutical company in Tennessee conceived the idea of preparing the drug in a liquid instead of a powder form and dissolved in diethylene glycol—a substance very much like anti-freeze for automobiles. It proved to be a costly and fatal preparation. Before its use could be stopped sixty-one people had died. A harmless lifesaving drug in one form became a fatal death-dealing potion in another form. It was not that they took something away from the drug that made sulphanilamide deadly. It was what they added. Error added to the truth becomes a deadly potion for the soul.

(2) *"Beware of evil workers."*

This is a further designation of the profane nature of the predatory and canine-like subversionists who had invaded Philippi, looking for prey. They were such as deceived by craft and skill and were in this respect different from the rapacious mongrels who debauched and devoured without culture and refinement. "These were workmen who with evil skill and craft, veneered error with the similitude of truth. They made what was partly wrong seem to be all right. They took the short linters of error and covered them with the sweet substance of truth. Evil workers indeed! Their breed is still among us in various cults and isms."

(3) *"Beware of the concision."*

This concludes the evil triad of devouring error, deceiving error and defiling error, all three characterizing the Judaizers who had invaded Philippi and who live today in their religious similitudes.

These concisionists or "flesh mutilators" advocated attachment to the law as a means of attaining the highest blessings of God. But Christianity is not something old: it is something new. It is not something obsolete: it is something current. It is not circumcision: it is regeneration. It is not body religion: it is character religion. It is not what you take off: it is what you put on.

Besides the more perilous forms of this legalism which exist today there are subtle and deceiving forms such as the artificial assumption that holiness consists of what you do not do, where you do not go and what you do not wear. But the emphasis of dynamic Christianity is on what you are. It is in the beauty of Christian character and not mere externalities only as the presence or absence of these reflect the essential beauty of Christ.

2. The Essentials of True Christianity. Verse 3.

"For we are the circumcision, which worship God
in the spirit, and rejoice in Christ Jesus, and have
no confidence in the flesh."

Here is a concise definitive statement of essential Christianity. It is what Paul chooses to call
the true circumcision. It is the new generation of
Spirit-born believers of grace. They were to be
distinguished from the legalists who depended
upon the additional and doubtful merits of body
religion.

True Christianity has three essentials:

(1) *Its worship—"in the Spirit."*

All true Christian worship begins within. It
is spiritual more than it is liturgical. It is of the
soul rather than of the senses. But it is equally
true that it does not end where it begins. If it
begins in the heart it is supposed to end with the
hands for "pure religion and undefiled before God
and the Father is this, To visit the fatherless and
widows in their affliction, and to keep himself un-
spotted from the world" (Jas. 1:27).

Christian worship "in the spirit," or more properly "by" the spirit, meant and end to the sacerdotal-
ism and ritualism of the Old Testament forms,
symbolism and typology. Since Christ's sacrifice
ended the old and began a new form of worship—
a worship which began within—it did not need the
things that appealed to the physical senses of see-
ing, feeling, hearing, smelling and tasting.

This new worship was an extension of the devotion of the worshipper from buildings and places, times and seasons, fasts and feasts, to the whole and total sphere of life. It was not seeking God in a special place, such as that place where the Shekinah glory of God dwelt; but finding God in every place.

This new worship was life communion with God upon a personal and immediate basis without benefit of priestly intermediaries or physical appliances. In fact, the word "worship" originally meant any sort of service, domestic or divine, sacred or secular (Moule). It was not intended to be something restricted to special places, special clothes and special ceremonies. It was life with God inspired and nurtured by a common gathering of His people for public and mutual expression of adoration to God.

Elton Trueblood tells the story of the stranger who slipped into a Quaker meeting and, becoming restless after a half hour of apparent inactivity, asked a fellow worshiper, "When does the service begin?" The answer came back, "The service begins when the meeting ends!" Perhaps the greatest evidence that there has been a meeting is the service that has begun. Zacchaeus made haste to come down and begin the service of repayment and unselfish living.

Any attempt to wrap Christianity in vestments, saturate it with incense, give it the sound of a dirge, sacerdotalize it and confine it to one building is not New Testament worship. Worship in the complete New Testament sense is spiritual and not ceremonial, joyful and not mournful, of the spirit and not of the flesh.

I still carry with me the remembrance of a man I once saw in Guatemala City. It was Sunday morning and I had just left the hotel to go to the great cathedral just across the square from the government building. Down the street beside the cathedral came this man. He wore a smart native jacket and well-washed cotton trousers with a wide-brimmed native hat at a jaunty angle. But the most conspicuous thing he wore was the smile on his face and the song from his lips and the reason was in the Bible he carried under his arm. He was on his way, not to the cathedral with its pomp and ceremony and lavish ornaments and priceless vestments and heavy-scented air and antiphonal singing and sacerdotal chanting and its bowing and genuflecting; but he was on his way to the little evangelical chapel down the street in an inconspicuous adobe building. I was sure when I saw him in what direction God could have been found in Guatemala City that Sunday morning, for this native was on his way to "worship God in the spirit."

(2) *Its glory—"rejoice in Christ Jesus."*

True Christianity is, as has been before stated, the life of Jesus Christ within us. This is the centrality of our faith—the person, the work and the continuing high priestly ministry of Jesus Christ.

(3) *Its principle—"no confidence in the flesh."*

It is elsewhere expressed by Paul to the Galatians, "I am crucified with Christ: nevertheless I live; yet not I, but Christ liveth in me: and the life which I now live in the flesh I live by the faith of the Son of God, who loved me, and gave himself for me" (Gal. 2:20).

The "flesh" is the equivalent of self or human nature "as fas as that word expresses that attitude or condition of our moral being which is not subject to God's law or reliant on His grace" (Moule). It is that part of our moral nature which is contrary to the nature and spirit of our new being.

The opposite of this confidence in the flesh is the confidence of faith which is the placing of all dependence of life upon the power of the inherent life of Christ. The difference between these two confidences is the difference between failure and success, mediocrity and greatness, fruitlessness and fruitfulness. Here are two ways of life. Whichever we choose for our way of life will determine what we will become.

III. THE CHRISTIAN'S TRUST. Verses 4-7.

> "Though I might also have confidence in the flesh. If any other man thinketh that he hath whereof he might trust in the flesh, I more: Circumcised the eighth day, of the stock of Israel, of the tribe of Benjamin, an Hebrew of the Hebrews; as touch-

> ing the law, a Pharisee; Concerning zeal, perse-
> cuting the church; touching the righteousness
> which is in the law, blameless. But what things
> were gain to me, those I counted loss for Christ."

The schismatic party which had attained a beachhead in Philippi advocated a system of religious externalism. These people depended upon tradition, ceremonials, visible appearances, pedigrees and all the things an external system boasts of.

Paul could summon as much to boast of and more. He could have built a very impressive standing of privilege and merit if this was what was necessary to have favor with God. So he says, "If any other man thinketh that he hath whereof he might trust in the flesh, I more" (vs. 4). He then proceeds to assemble his religious heritage and pedigree item by item, excellence by excellence, merit by merit. Then when it is finished he destroys this house of religious insecurity in which he could have lived by saying, "But what things were gain to me, those I counted loss for Christ. Yea doubtless, and I count all things but loss for the excellency of the knowledge of Christ Jesus my Lord" (vss. 7, 8). All of these things vanish into nothing before his vital position as a Christian.

Here are the seven specifics of Paul's religious pedigree which, if it could save, would have brought Saul of Tarsus an abundant salvation.

1. Pride of Tradition. Verse 5.

"Circumcised the eighth day."

Paul was not a proselyte brought in as an adult from another persuasion. He was a traditional religionist who wore the badge of his faith from infancy.

2. Pride of Birth. Verse 5.

"Of the stock of Israel."

Paul was a blood-born Jew. He belonged to the original religious aristocracy. The personal defense of many people who are approached about their personal relationship to God is often that of pride of ancestry. Ancestors can leave us many things including property, money, memories and wisdom but they cannot bequeath their virtue, righteousness or salvation. These must be acquired in our own right.

It is not the blood of ancestors which saves but the blood of Christ. It is not an age encrusted family name that saves but the name of Jesus for "there is none other name under heaven given among men, whereby we must be saved" (Acts 4:12).

3. Pride of Position. Verse 5.

"Of the tribe of Benjamin."

Among Israelites the Benjaminites were particularly distinguished like the Cabots and the Standishes.

Are there noble traditions of position and fame in your family? Then thank God. Be justly proud of them if you will. But trust in none of them to give you excellence before God for none of these things accrue to moral credit before the great judge of all men. You are on your own before Him on the basis of that very narrow strip of time between the date of your birth and the date of your death.

4. Pride of Caste. Verse 5.

"An Hebrew of the Hebrews."

At Philippi there were Hellenistic Jews who had dropped the language and manners and customs of Jewry and conformed themselves to Greek ideals and customs. It was not true of Paul who was still Hebraically Hebrew. He had not lost caste.

The Cross of Christ is the great leveling place of life. There are no great men or rich men or wise men or mighty men or distinguished men. There are only sinful men needing a Saviour who can bring them out of all the artificial distinctions of culture and religion and into the family of God.

5. Pride of Religion. Verse 5.

"As touching the law, a Pharisee."

Paul belonged to the party of religious conformists as opposed to the rationalistic Sadducees and the political Herodians and the fanatical Zealots. He believed in religious regularity. He was a Democrat of the Democrats, a Republican of the Republicans in his religious party affiliation. But even religious regularity could not save and this too had to go upon the dung hill of cast-off pedigrees.

Once an old woman, asked if she had religion, replied, "No, thank God, I've lost that, it was nearly the death of me, and now I have Christ." I would to God that the multitude of our religionists today would make the same fruitful exchange.

6. Pride of Reputation. Verse 6.

"Concerning zeal, persecuting the church."

He measured his religious zeal by his hatred of Christians. Before a God of love hatred is never a credential of salvation, even though there are legitimate objects to be hateful of.

We may do this same thing in a different way— *Christians* measuring their Christianity by their hatred of communism, *Fundamentalists* measuring their orthodoxy by their hatred of modernism, *Protestants* measuring their Protestantism by their hatred of Catholicism. It is a precarious reputation indeed which is measured by such standards. The only standard of excellence and durability is Christ. He survives every test.

7. Pride of Character. Verse 6.

"Touching the righteousness which is in the law, blameless."

It is doubtful whether Paul was claiming the ultimate and perfect moral fulfillment of the law but rather the observance of its literal and external requirements. Even so, it was not sufficient for one day came the supreme test of moral perfection. It was on the Damascus Road when Saul of Tarsus met the Christ of God and then all of these boasted dependencies vanished in His presence. And there in the presence of Christ Paul made this life-changing decision, "But what things were gain to me, those I counted loss for Christ."

Paul did not come out of one religious experience into another religious experience. He suffered "loss" but he experienced "gain." He exchanged religion for Christ. Christianity is Christ and whosoever is willing to surrender the imagined credits and merits of self-acquired righteousness for Christ will secure the immutable benefits of a moral and spiritual righteousness that are the equal of Christ's.

Paul suffered loss that he might find gain. Paul stepped out of himself and was brought into Christ. It is this of which the poet speaks when he says:

"Out of disaster and ruin complete,
  Out of the struggle and dreary defeat,
  Out of my sorrow, and burden, and shame,
  Out of the evils too fearful to name,
  Out of my guilt and the criminal's doom,
  Out of the dread, and the terror, and gloom:
  Into the sense of forgiveness and rest,
  Into inheritance with all the blest,
  Into a righteous and permanent peace,
  Into the grandest and fullest release—
  Into a comfort without an alloy,
  Into a perfect and confident joy.
      Wonderful holiness, bringing to light!
      Wonderful grace, putting all out of sight!

    Wonderful wisdom, devising the way!
    Wonderful power that nothing could stay.
Out of the horror of being alone,
Out, and forever, of being my own,
Out of the hardness of heart and of will,
Out of the longings which nothing could fill—
Out of the bitterness, madness, and strife,
Out of myself and all I called life:
Into communion with Father and Son,
Into the sharing of all that Christ won,
Into the ecstacies, full to the brim,
Into the having of all things with Him,
Into Christ Jesus, there ever to dwell,
Into more blessing than words can e'er tell.
    Wonderful lowliness draining my cup!
    Wonderful purpose that ne'er gave me up!
    Wonderful patience that waited so long!
    Wonderful glory to which I belong!"

IV. THE CHRISTIAN'S DESIRE. Verses 8-11.

"Yea doubtless, and I count all things but loss for the excellency of the knowledge of Christ Jesus my Lord: for whom I have suffered the loss of all things, and do count them but dung, that I may win Christ, and be found in him, not having mine own righteousness, which is of the law, but that which is through the faith of Christ, the righteousness which is of God by faith: That I may know him, and the power of his resurrection, and the fellowship of his sufferings, being made conformable unto his death; if by any means I might attain unto the resurrection of the dead."

Here is the true Christian philosophy of life. Here is doctrine in its purest form. Here is life to its best advantage. Here is the *summum bonum* of the Christian faith.

What Paul had counted loss were not evil things. They were in the nature of personal attainments in competition to the saving righteousness of Jesus Christ. They were all good things but not good enough and when salvation is at stake, a good thing becomes a bad thing if it becomes a substitute for the best thing.

There are some who stand in the guilt of their own choosing because they, too, are allowing the excellencies of their self-chosen righteousness to become a substitute for the only way that can save—the righteousness of Jesus Christ. Not until these say what Paul said can they find what he found. He said, "Yea doubtless, and I count all things but loss for the excellency of the knowledge of Christ Jesus my Lord: for whom I have suffered the loss of all things, and do count them but dung, that I may win Christ."

This renunciation of Paul brings three great objects of desire into view. In verse 8 it is *to win Christ*. In verse 9 it is *to be found in Christ*. In verse 10 it is *to know Christ*. In verse 8 it is *the Person* of this new relationship. In verse 9 it is *the Position* of this new relationship. In verse 10 it is *the Power* of this new relationship.

We will look at them seriatim:

1. The Desire to "win Christ." *The Person of Salvation*. Verse 8.

" . . . I have suffered the loss of all things, and
do count them but refuse, that I may win Christ."

Paul had found the source and secret of all the
benefits and blessings of salvation. All that God
wants us to have for time and eternity are potentially
and positionally provided for us and available to us
in the person of Jesus Christ. Find Him and you
will find everything.

2. The Desire to be "found in Christ." *The Position of Salvation.* Verse 9.

"And be found in him, not having mine own righteousness, which is of the law, but that which is
through the faith of Christ, the righteousness which
is of God by faith."

In this position we are saved: out of it we are
lost. In it we receive the benefits of Christ's
righteousness : out of it we must trust in our own
righteousness. One is the righteousness of the law.
The other is the righteousness of faith. One righteousness leads to condemnation. The other righteousness leads to justification.

3. The Desire to "know Him." *The Power of Salvation.* Verses 10, 11.

"That I may know him, and the power of his resurrection, and the fellowship of his sufferings, being
made comfortable unto his death: If by any
means I might attain unto the resurrection of the
dead."

The order of experience as given here is the order of Christian experience, not the order of salvation. In the order of salvation and Christ's passion it was suffering, death and resurrection, but in the order of the Christian life it is resurrection, suffering and death.

(1) *To know Him in "the power of His resurrection."*

In the formula of faith found in Romans 10:9, 10 faith in the resurrection is described as the first item of a saving faith: "That if thou . . . shalt believe in thine heart that God hath raised him from the dead, thou shalt be saved." It is faith in the resurrection at this point, not the crucifixion, because the resurrection authenticates and verifies the purpose of the crucifixion and provides justification. Upon the realization of this faith come life for the resurrection releases to every believer in Jesus the life He died to give.

(2) *To know Him in "the fellowship of His sufferings."*

Consider His sufferings and then ponder an experience of fellowship in those sufferings. Those sufferings included the temptation of Satan, the deprivations of daily life, inhumanities from his enemies, denial at the hands of friends, betrayal by an associate, misunderstanding by men at large, hatred by the privileged class, and at last the agonies of a terrible death. Are you ready to pray this prayer now?

Suffering for the sake of Christ is another form of participation in Christ's sufferings. (*See I Pet. 4:13.*)

Paul has not written here all that this fellowship involves but it is a dangerous prayer to pray unless we are willing to accept the fullest implications and consequences of it. A man who often said "I'd give my right arm" to see his ailing daughter cured lost the arm in a car crash—and she was mysteriously healed. The odd case, with the names withheld, was described by Dr. J. M. H. Smellie of Liverpool in a recent issue of the *British Medical Journal.* Dr. Smellie said the girl was crippled by arthritis and disfigured by a skin disease associated with it. Her devoted father tried all kinds of treatment but she did not respond. One day he set off on a motor trip with the girl and his wife. The car was wrecked and the father's right arm was torn off. Before his wound had healed, the daughter's skin trouble and arthritis had vanished. Dr. Smellie offered two possible explanations—the cure might have been due to psychological factors or to cortisone liberated from the girl's adrenal glands by the shock of the accident. In time of shock the adrenal glands, situated near the kidneys, pour out cortisone. This substance has come to the fore in recent years in the treatment of arthritis.

If there is power for us in the resurrection of Christ there is also fellowship of the richest character in His sufferings, and when we "know Him" to the limit of that knowledge we will know the greatest and most enriching experiences of the Christian life.

(3) *To know Him in "the conformation of His death."*

Here is spiritual identification with Christ in His death in which we can say, "I am crucified with Christ . . ." There must be a likeness to Him in His death before there can be a likeness to Him in His life; for life in the Christian order always arises out of death. Birth is always in the shadow of death. Life is sustained only by things that have died for we eat only what is dead.

To know Christ in the fullest extent of knowledge is to know Him in the power of His resurrection in the kinship and fellowship of His sufferings and in the likeness of His death. And when these three things are put together they add up to a spiritual relationship to and experience with Christ in the highest expression of His advent—the fruits of redemption.

Is it not all too true that most of us enjoy the fellowship of Christ's blessings and shun the fellowship of His sufferings? Yet only through suffering is character perfected and life's highest purpose realized. Oh God, give us we pray thee a prayer purpose that will enable us to "know him, and the power of his resurrection, and the fellowship of his sufferings, being made conformable unto his death."

The culminating desire to which the preceding desires lead us is in verse 11: "If by any means I might attain unto the resurrection of the dead." The desire is not one of doubt that Paul will attain a personal resurrection but one of humility that he is unworthy of such a resurrection and therefore he is willing to share in the power of Christ's resurrection now and experience the fellowship of Christ's sufferings now and be made conformable to Christ's death now that he may be fit to share in the resurrection later.

The resurrection to which Paul aspires is the resurrection of those who comprise the Body of Christ in distinction from those who do not. For those who do not there will be a resurrection in the closing phases of world history. Here is an out-resurrection or a resurrection from among the dead which will leave some still in the state of death. It will occur at the time of Christ's return and is to be followed by the parousia which is described in the language of I Thessalonians 4:13-18.

Christianity is often criticized as an impractical, other-worldly religious experience which puts desires of future bliss and ease first in life to the exclusion of practical earthly considerations. That this is not true is seen in Paul's great desires for life attainments. Here he had linked his desires for the future with his duty in the present. With this desire he is determined not to neglect the obligations and duties of his present life. The future and its resurrection is an aspiration which provides an inspiration for the living of his present life.

V. The Christian's Goal. Verses 12-14.

> "Not as though I had already attained, either were already perfect: but I follow after, if that I may apprehend that for which also I am apprehended of Christ Jesus. Brethren, I count not myself to have apprehended: but this one thing I do, forgetting those things which are behind, and reaching forth unto those things which are before, I press toward the mark for the prize of the high calling of God in Christ Jesus."

Paul states his own spiritual condition and aspiration in the words of verse 12. "Not as though I had already attained, either were already perfect."

Paul rejects the idea of a theoretical Christian perfection as already attained in the realm of conduct and action. In verse 11 he expresses his desires to "attain unto the resurrection of the dead." In verse 12 he describes a state in which he is presently found: "Not as though I had already attained." In verse 11 the attainment is a goal which he has not reached, which is resurrection perfection. In verse 12 the attainment is an active appropriation which he has not made. He confesses that while he has experienced God's power surging through his life to some degree, yet he has not appropriated the fullest measure of its possibilities. He was spiritually realistic and, we might add, honest. But he also says, "either were already perfect." This is not a state which means sinless or flawless. It means "spiritually mature" and the apostle is telling us that he is not professing to have come to a place in his Christian life where his growth is complete and where there is no further room for advancement.

We must remember that Paul was positionally perfect in Christ while being conditionally perfected in both character and conduct. In his position Paul was complete, finished and perfect. In his condition Paul was striving to know Christ in the power of His resurrection, in the fellowship of His sufferings, in the conformation of His death.

Paul next states his present spiritual purpose: "But I follow after, if that I may apprehend that for which also I am apprehended of Christ Jesus." And going on he says, "Brethren, I count not myself to have apprehended [*made it my own*]: but this one thing I do." He determines to apprehend that for which he has been apprehended; to lay hold of that for which he has been laid hold; to make his own that for which Christ made him His own.

For what purpose had Christ made Paul His own? The answer is Bible-wide. It is even prehistoric. It is that Paul should become like Jesus Christ. It is that he and we should "be conformed to the image of his son." This moral and spiritual likeness to Christ is the ultimate goal expressed in four ways in this very chapter. In verse 8—*to win Christ*. In verse 9—*to be found in Christ.* In verse 10—*to know Christ.* In verse 21—*to be like Christ.*

Yes, there is purpose in Christian experience. It is first God's purpose to conform us to the image of His Son. Then it should be our purpose to be conformed to that image through the means of grace God places at our disposal. When we become Christians it is the beginning rather than the end of a purpose. That purpose is the ultimate transformation of all the parts of the human personality into the character likeness of Jesus Christ. The achievement of this purpose is the highest aspiration of Christian idealism. It is so important to Paul that He makes it the primary objective of his life and says, "this one thing I do." Here is both consecration and concentration. In fact, consecration is simply concentration upon a single goal—the goal of Christian holiness and righteousness as found in Christ. Here is achievement within the grasp of all. It does not require great ability, great knowledge or great prestige but simply great determination—"this one thing I do." The word impossible does not exist for the Christian who says, "this one thing I do." Though he may be unlearned, poor, deficient, aged, weak or sick, if he purposes and pursues this ideal he will ultimately arrive at the place of moral and spiritual excellence.

Demosthenes, born with a serious speech defect, became the greatest of all orators. He determined to correct his defect and did so by speaking with pebbles in his mouth against the roar of the ocean at surfside. It is a greater achievement to become a humble Christian who can speak by life and lip the living gospel of the living Christ than to become the greatest orator.

There now appears the threefold secret of Paul's life and ours too if we will adopt it.

1. "Forgetting those things which are behind." Verse 13.

This deals with the *past*.

None will ever reach the heights of a great life until he has dealt with the past. Paul's formula is to "forget." But forgetting the past is not done by mental magic with a Houdini's wand; nor by a psychological trick. It is dealt with by an ethical principle found in redemption. It does not mean that we can cross out and cancel the past by wishful thinking and go on from any given point as though the past never existed. It means the forgetfulness that comes by confession, correction and restitution. This is the only successful way forgetfulness can wipe out an unfortunate past.

We must deal with the past or the past will deal with us. Our past has the faculty of becoming our present unless we discharge our obligation to it. Our confession and God's forgiveness is the only sure way to obliterate and annihilate the past. And unless we get rid of it, it will get rid of us. Unless we treat it thus, it will become a haunting memory to sap our strength, dog our footsteps and handicap our life. Liquidate your liabilities for unless you do you will carry them over into any new beginning you try to make.

Pause with me a moment. Have you dealt with your past? Or is it still with you as a bitter memory, a gnawing pain in your spiritual vitals like the young stoic who stole a fox and hid it under his tunic when his superior officer suddenly appeared, and stoic that he was, let that fox tear out his vital organs so that he dropped dead. Is your past still alive? Get rid of it, not psychologically, but spiritually through confession and correction.

One way to forget your past is not to repeat your mistakes. It is not so serious to make a mistake as to repeat it. I am reminded of the rather humorous story of the little boy at the theater with his mother. Danny was taken to see the movie, "Snow White and the Seven Dwarfs." They entered the theater during the middle of the picture just before the old witch gave Snow White the poisoned apple. When they came to the same part again, Danny's mother arose and began to lead him out of the theater. As they were leaving, Danny looked back to see the old witch offering Snow White the poisoned apple. Danny said to his mother, "If Snow White eats that apple again, she's crazy!"

Another way to forget your past is not to become historical. A man met an old college friend downtown one night. They sat down in the lobby of the hotel and began to talk over old times. Before they realized it, it was long past midnight. They went on home, but both of them were a little fearful of what their wives would say about their coming in so late. The next day they met again. One asked, "How did your wife take your coming in so late?" "Oh," the other replied, "I explained it to her and it was all right. What about your wife?"

"Well," he said, "when I came in my wife got historical." "You mean 'hysterical,' don't you?" his friend asked. "No," he said, "I mean 'historical.' She brought up everything that has happened the past thirty years."

When Winston Churchill visited the United States during the war years he remarked in the course of a conversation, "If the present quarrels with the past, there can be no future." If your present is quarreling with your past you can have no future.

There are many specifics of memory which should be forgotten; our grievances, our hurts, our sorrows, our sins and all the host of things that trail us from yesterday into tomorrow to make us miserable instead of happy.

2. "Reaching forth unto those things which are before." Verse 13.

This concerns the *present*.

Life should have both motion and direction. Let us go on. Let us go forward. Obliterate the past and activate the present; these are the essentials of attainment.

These "things which are before" are included in the previously expressed ideal of attaining the perfection of Christian character which is Christlikeness and the perfection of character.

3. "I press toward the mark for the prize of the high calling of God in Christ Jesus." Verse 14.

This concerns the *future*.

Toward the past—*forget*. Toward the present—*advance*. Toward the future—*persevere*.

What is the prize for which we should persevere? It is not heaven for heaven is not a prize won by our merits or efforts. Heaven is God's gift of grace and will be the last of the three phases of regeneration which are a new man, a new body and a new world. It is not salvation, for salvation is likewise not a prize to be won by merits and efforts. Furthermore salvation is not an attainment of the future but a possession of the present.

Paul is cast here in the role of a runner. He is in the race and the prize is the victor's wreath characteristic of the Grecian games. It could refer therefore to the crown of victory, the runner's wreath and the victor's prize Paul refers to in II Timothy 4:7,8. "As for me, I think my work is done. I am as wine just about to be spilt on the altar—as a ship at point to put out to sea. I am a wrestler who has striven through a gallant struggle, a runner who has finished his race, a soldier who has kept his oath of loyal obedience. Henceforth there is laid up in store for me the victor's wreath of righteousness, which the Lord will award me in the Great Day, the Lord the Righteous Judge—and not to me alone, but to all who with yearning love have watched for His appearing" (Arthur S. Way's Translation). It is the prize of a well-fought fight, a well-run race and a well-kept trust. It is the ultimate of life's goals, the highest achievement of Christian experience. It is the prize "of the high calling [the upward call] of God in Christ Jesus."

Where are you at this moment—on the race course in competition or in the stadium as a spectator? In the fight as a contestant or on the sidelines as an observer? Keeping a trust or with empty hands interested in your own pursuits? Some day you will regret this indolence, this spectator Christianity, this contribution-less profession which does no service and produces no fruit; but lives only for self.

VI. The Christian's Walk. Verses 15-19.

"Let us therefore, as many as be perfect, be thus minded: and if in any thing ye be otherwise minded, God shall reveal even this unto you. Nevertheless, whereto we have already attained, let us walk by the same rule, let us mind the same thing. Brethren, be followers together of me, and mark them which walk so as ye have us for an ensample. (For many walk, of whom I have told you often, and now tell you even weeping, that they are the enemies of the cross of Christ: Whose end is destruction, whose God is their belly, and whose glory is in their shame, who mind earthly things.)"

Here are the humble realities of our daily life. We are brought down from the celestial aspects of our high calling to the earthly responsibilities of life and from the ideals of Christian perfection to the realities of Christian progress. Our walk is the last argument of our faith. It is not "every one that saith unto me, Lord, Lord [that] shall enter into the kingdom of heaven; but he that doeth the will of my Father which is in heaven" (Matt. 7:21).

The New Testament provides us with a heavenly model for our earthly walk. This model is in terms of principle and not in the interminable specifics of detailed action. If we respect the model we will be saved from two extremes:

1. The Extreme of Perfectionism. Verses 15,16.

"Let us therefore, as many as be perfect, be thus minded: and if in any thing ye be otherwise minded, God shall reveal even this unto you. Nevertheless, whereto we have already attained, let us walk by the same rule, let us mind the same thing."

It is often assumed that when the Bible uses the word perfect it always means flawless and sinless behavior. But flawlessness can never be properly associated with behavior in a human being. It is applied to our relationship to Christ. In this context it means moral ripeness, Christian maturity or being full grown and sound. Paul has already spoken of himself in verse 12 as being perfect but not perfected. He is perfect before God while being perfected before man.

It is like an apple, as someone has conceived it. In June it is a perfect apple but in September it is a perfected apple. In June it is perfect as a horticultural specimen but in September it is perfected as a full grown, beautifully colored and deliciously tasting specimen of refined fruit. In June it is progressing in perfection. In September it is perfect in progress. So is the Christian—perfect in standing and being perfected in state and experience.

But, this is not an automatic and impersonal perfection. It requires our acceptance and the application of the means of grace. No more can a Christian grow in the perfection of maturity without respecting his spiritual environment than can an apple without its environment of natural law. And as one looks about him in the church there are a good many sour, scrawny apples clinging to God's tree of life.

2. The Extreme of Antinomianism.
Verses 17-19.

"Brethren, be followers together of me, and mark them which walk so as ye have us for an ensample. (For many walk, of whom I have told you often, and now tell you even weeping, that they are the enemies of the cross of Christ: Whose end is

destruction, whose God is their belly, and whose
glory is in their shame, who mind earthly things.)"

Antinomianism is a theological term fashioned
from two words, anti-—against, and nomian—law.
It sponsors the extreme and false idea that since
grace has come and the law has gone there is no
responsibility to keep its moral requirements. It
argues that since there are no rules there can be
no regulations. Hence, one may do what he likes
for in doing what he likes he is not subject to any
judgment for what he does. To answer this dangerous doctrine we have only to remember that faith
without works is dead. So is creed without conduct. So are words without walk. So is preaching
without practice.

If the ceremonial and civil and specifically
nationalistic aspects of the law of Moses are abro-
gated, set aside and completed in Christ, it is still
true that the moral requirements of the law are as
binding and obligatory as ever. For these remain
as much in grace as in law—as much in Christ as in
Moses—as much in Romans as Leviticus—as much
in the New Testament as the Old Testament.

Paul reduces the question of Christian behavior to its simplest terms—*an example.* He says,
"Brethren, be followers together of me, and mark
them which walk so as ye have us for an ensample"
(vs. 17). Here it is not rules, laws, regulations but
experience, demonstration, proof and evidence. It
has worked for me, says Paul, and it will work for

you. Paul is more than a life-size model—he is a Christ-size model. His was not showcase religion but laboratory experience. He had lived it in the silence of Arabia, the synagogue of Antioch, the stoning at Lystra, the maelstrom at Ephesus and now the incarceration at Rome. Paul's example is proof that Christ is real and Christianity works—"follow me."

The greatest hindrance to the progress of Christianity in any century is internal, not external. Caesar, Hadrian, Diocletian and their pagan contemporaries were formidable enemies. But a vital and vibrant Christianity swept them into the limbo of oblivion while it marches on. The real peril to Christianity is inside; in its wolves who wear the sheep's clothing of the ministry; in its members who wear the second face of hypocrites; in those who speak its language and profess its truth but are in the essence "the enemies of the Cross of Christ" because they do not live its life by demonstrating its truth in honesty, purity and morality.

None of the traditionally great and outspoken enemies of Christianity like Hadrian, Voltaire, Bolingbroke, Payne and Ingersol ever inflicted such great havoc upon the church as these internal enemies whose profession is wanting in sincerity and purity.

All of this turns back upon a simple phrase of great meaning in verse 16—*"Let us walk."* Jesus Christ is the object of our walk, the companion of our walk, the inspiration of our walk and the reward of our walk. *"Let us walk."* Jesus said, "I must walk today and tomorrow and the day following." So must we. He walked toward the Cross. We walk with the Cross. *"Let us walk."* "As ye have therefore received Christ Jesus the Lord, so *walk* ye in him."

VII. THE CHRISTIAN'S HOPE. Verses 20, 21.

> "For our conversation is in heaven; from whence also we look for the Saviour, the Lord Jesus Christ: Who shall change our vile body, that it may be fashioned like unto his glorious body, according to the working whereby he is able even to subdue all things unto himself."

We come again upon the word "conversation" the meaning of which relates to our life's walk which is here described as being heavenly in its model, ideal, origin and destiny.

Any person's good walk requires a number of things. It requires *position*—a place to begin; *motion*—a power with which to live; *direction*—a course upon which to move; *posture*—an attitude in which to live; *fashion*—a form of life in which we appear; *destination*—a goal toward which we move.

Posture is an important part of any person's walk. He who has a bad posture presents a bad appearance. He who stoops will become stunted and misshapen with cavernous chest, sloping shoulders and slovenly gait. The posture of our Christian walk is equally important. Paul has just observed that many were walking unworthily, minding earthly things, with their appetites as their gods. Consequently this bad posture gave them a deformed walk with its ill effects upon those who watched them. To counteract bad moral and spiritual posture Paul says, "our conversation is in heaven." Heaven is the center of gravitation for our moral and spiritual lives. Heaven is the seat of our citizenship. Every true Christian is a citizen of heaven "enrolled on its registers, possessed of its privileges, awaiting its destiny" and some day he will be surrounded with its glory. In the meantime he is "obliged by the nobility of such a position to live . . . as those who belong to it and represent it." Hence the citizen-Christian patterns his life after the ideals of heaven and so long as he does he saves himself from the dangers of a contemporary society of earth-bound pagans.

In the light of heaven no possession, no trait of character, no characteristic of conduct, no acquired habit is worth the possession or retention if it cannot be translated into heavenly property. When Captain Eddie Rickenbacker and his companions of the ill-fated air expedition in the South Seas prepared to abandon their plane they threw out everything that was movable. "In the face of death," Captain Rickenbacker has since said, "if you ever think that material things are worth anything, ladies and gentlemen, have that experience and you will find out how useless they are, no matter how you may have cherished them." Let us learn the lesson before death forces it upon us.

We not only have our *life* from heaven but we behold the prospect of our *Lord* from heaven—"from whence also we look for the Saviour, the Lord Jesus Christ." It is a strange twisting of words which makes Christ's coming to us our going to Him. Since when does coming mean going? Only when down means up and black means white.

The earliest Christians looked for Christ's return. They did it upon the basis of His visible departure. "Ye men of Galilee, why stand ye gazing up into heaven? this same Jesus, which is taken up from you into heaven, shall so come in like manner as ye have seen him go into heaven" (Acts 1:11). We modern Christians look for Christ's return upon the basis of His verbal promise. The effect of this coming will be twofold:

1. To Change our Bodies. Verse 21.

> "Who shall change our vile body, that it may be
> fashioned like unto his glorious body, according to
> the working whereby he is able even to subdue all
> things unto himself."

Our present bodies are described as "vile." Our coming bodies are described as being "glori-

ous." The difference between being vile and glorious is the coming of Christ and the second state
of redemption, which is a new body. Our present
bodies are not "vile" in the sense of their organic
construction, nor in the sense of their flesh. It refers to their lowly nature in contrast to their coming
glory. It further refers to their link with the lower
creatures and the relationship with the curse coming
by sin.

The body has an inherited accumulation of
past sins. It is subject to disease and death. It
must be worn with handicap and liability. It has
only a limited field of expression. We cannot express the full nature of our spiritual life by our
present bodies. But this will be changed in the
glorification because if there has been regeneration and justification and sanctification, there will
also be glorification as the final phase of our redemptive experience.

God assigns to the body, in this Christian doctrine of eschatology, a destiny hitherto unknown in
the ancient world. In Paul's day they conceived
the body to be a prison of the spirit which would
be dropped, disintegrated and destroyed at death.
But in the Christian concept and economy the body
is to become the counterpart of the spirit and is to
continue in glorified form as the vehicle of the
spirit's expression.

This is perfectly plausible for if we have a
new manhood now through regeneration and are

to have a new world through renovation, it will be necessary in that new environment to have a new body, inasmuch as heaven is a place and requires a body for the Spirit's manifestation.

The *change* in the body will take place at the return of Christ.

The *process of the change* at His return will be twofold. It will be resurrection for those who are dead. It will be translation for those who are alive. Both resurrection and translation shall change the body from its present state of humiliation to its destined state of glorification.

The *nature of the change* will be an exchange, for vileness will be exchanged for glory and humiliation will be exchanged for exaltation.

The *pattern of the change* will be "his glorious body" so that we will have a body of material (spiritual) substance which can be handled, seen, receive nourishment, have unlimited mobility and locomotion and be without limit of space or time. It will possess all the senses we have at present but in higher degrees of perfection. It will have the necessity for food since there is a Tree of Life of which to partake. It will possess the power of unobstructed flight, overcoming all the forces of time and space. It will possess great celerity of motion with a velocity unknown or undreamed by any of our known standards of flight.

The *description of the change* is in I Corinthians 15:54, "So when this corruptible shall have put on incorruption, and this mortal shall have put on immortality, then shall be brought to pass the saying that is written, Death is swallowed up in victory."

The *preview of the change* is given once in Matthew 17:1,2 and once in II Corinthians 12:1-4.

The *character of the change* is indicated in the language Paul uses—"who shall change." This change means "to make of another form" and indicates a complete transformation in substance and ability. In this connection none of the Scriptures argue for a resurrection of all the molecules of our present body as if there had to be a gathering together of every part of this present body. It is the germ of the old body which provides the beginning of the new body. We expect a resurrection of the body not a resurrection of the flesh. The Bible nowhere calls for the resurrection of our flesh and bones, only of a body which will be transformed into another form.

2. To Subdue All Things. Verse 21.

> "Who shall change our vile body, that it may be fashioned like unto his glorious body, according to the working whereby, he is able even to subdue all things unto himself."

The word "subdue" is not the ordinary word for subjection or subjugation, but a word indicating that a disordered world and its universal environs will be set in order—actually it means *to set in array.*

It is what sometimes happens in your home. You go to the store or away on an errand and when you come back the living room has been rearranged in the imagined form of a train with a long line of chairs, tables and other furniture making up the train. You come home and set it in order. You "subdue all things." You subdue the disorder and disarrangement of childish minds. You put each piece of furniture in its place. You restore the whole house to your personal, orderly authority. This is precisely what is going to happen when Christ returns. He will proceed to arrange this disordered world system. Humanity's furniture will be put in place. The spears and swords of war now understood as tanks and bazookas and jet planes and battleships will be beaten into the pruninghooks and plowshares of peaceful implements.

In the Smithsonian Institute at Washington, is on exhibit a miniature plowshare made as a paper weight from materials of war by the late William Jennings Bryan. Similar paper weights were presented in 1918 to thirty diplomats who signed treaties providing for the investigation of all disputes. Upon them were carved the Scripture: "They shall beat their swords into plowshares, and their spears into pruninghooks." At Christ's return, however, it will be more than a sentiment. He is going to break up the bloody games of war and start a school of peace. All these adolescent men who have been making such a mess of this world He will put directly under His authority. Here is the ultimate solution of world problems. We do not and cannot solve them by inventions of science or by our educational processes; these only increase our problems. It can only be done under divine authority.

Men now live by squatter's rights upon God's earth. He is its legal owner. We are here by sufferance. We rule under divine franchise; and when the full measure of divine mercy is reached Christ will return to do what we have failed to do. He will set in array. He will establish a universal rule. It will be a government never known before for its absolute justice, absolute equity, absolute righteousness and undisturbed security.

What is your prospect of a place and participation in this coming order? To have a place in the changed world you too must be changed. The order or disorder of your life must be made subject to the will of God. Preparation for participation must come through regeneration.

4

THE CHRISTIAN'S PEACE IN LIFE
Philippians 1

THE PREVIOUS chapter struck a high note of truth by setting before us the objectives of the Christian life. The primary objective was Jesus Christ, in whose presence and by whose possession we could reach the high places of character and usefulness. This chapter begins with a "therefore." It was once remarked by a wise old minister that when one came upon the word "therefore" in the Scriptures he ought to stop and see what it was *there for.* Here it is "a conclusion drawn from what precedes," namely that in Jesus Christ is the great object of life while in our human leaders, such as Paul, are the human examples for that life. Paul has said (3:17), "Brethren, be followers together of me, and mark them which walk so as ye have us for an ensample." With this in mind he turns to his final considerations of the advancing life of the Christian.

The dominant word of this chapter is "peace" —verse 7. It is the primary teaching of this Scripture. It takes precedence over every other consideration. In all the search of men there is nothing he seems to desire more than peace of mind and a tranquil and happy state of life. We are here taught how it may be obtained.

The president of one of our major motor car companies stated that at the time he was speaking the intrinsic value of an automobile was only $24.00. The final cost of an automobile, however, was at that time around $2500 to $3000. The difference between the intrinsic value of the rubber, ore, sand, metals, etc. and the actual value was the cost of labor, manufacture and advertising plus profits. On the basis of this amazing fact we observe what is likewise true in human life. It is not the intrinsic physical, material, social and circumstantial values that count most. The intrinsic value of the materials in a man's body used to be ninety-eight cents. As a result of inflation it is now $31.04. This is what it would cost to buy the components of his body at the corner drugstore. But the body is not our life. Nor is it clothes or comforts or luxuries that make up the actual and true value of life. Life consists of faith, righteousness, courage, peace, godliness, eternity, faithfulness and fruitfulness. In other words, the difference between the intrinsic value of the physical components of life and the actual value of life's ultimate objectives is life's workmanship and investments.

In the preamble to our Constitution are the words: "We hold these truths to be self-evident, that all men are created equal, that they are endowed by their Creator with certain inalienable rights, that among these are life, liberty, and the pursuit of happiness." Happiness, however, is not a pursuit: it is a possession. It is not a right that is realized by virtue of citizenship. It will be realized by the respect we have for divine laws as those laws operate in the mind and in the circumstances of the child of God.

It is possible to achieve a certain measure of peace of mind through human agencies. The inspiration of books, the application of psychological factors all would produce a certain measure of peace; but we are dealing here, not with men's peace of mind, but God's peace of heart. Here is that lasting, sufficient and continuing experience that comes from the Christian's relationship with God.

Peace as an abiding possession of the heart is related to four things: to God, to prayer, to the mind and to our circumstances. These constitute the components of this chapter.

I. PEACE AND ITS RELATIONSHIP TO GOD. Verses 1-4.

"Therefore, my brethren dearly beloved and longed for, my joy and crown, so stand fast in the Lord, my dearly beloved. I beseech Euodias, and beseech Syntyche, that they be of the same mind in the Lord. And I intreat thee also, true yokefellow, help those women which laboured with me in the gospel, with Clement also, and with other my fellowlabourers, whose names are in the book of life. Rejoice in the Lord alway: and again I say, Rejoice."

The real key to this section lies immediately beyond it in verse 5 where it says, "The Lord is at hand." This was a watchword of Philippian faithfulness and steadfastness. Two equally true and important meanings will be found in these words. First, "the Lord is at hand" in His parousia or second coming. This is the primary meaning because to be at "hand" meant "near" in point of time and expectation and referred no doubt to the Rapture. It was undoubtedly true that the understanding of the imminent return of Christ was a stabilizing incentive in the early Church. It became the constant source of power and peace. If we could speak of anything else as offering a greater assurance of peace and stability than the nearness of the Lord's return, it was the assurance of Christ's continuing and constant presence in His Church in a spiritual sense. This is the second meaning of the phrase, "the Lord is at hand." This concept of the Lord's relationship to His people would not lessen the importance of the advent truth. It would, however, invest the present life with the larger influence that all of life should be lived in the immediate presence of Christ. This would stimulate sanctity and sincerity since all life was under the personal scrutiny of Jesus Christ. In this concept the Lord's presence was not in a future event but in a present fact. The future event would some day bring climax to the present fact.

Think what this must have meant to Paul in prison at Rome. The fact that "the Lord is at hand" overshadowed every other consideration and compensated for every disadvantage Paul endured. It, in effect, crumbled prison walls, melted prison doors and dispersed prison guards. The reality of a prison dissolved in the overwhelming presence of Christ.

Think what this must have meant to the Christians at Philippi! It more than compensated for every sacrifice. It gave sufficiency in every demanding situation. To be sure, Philippi was still Philippi, even as Rome was still Rome, but this Roman outpost at the periphery of the empire was transformed into a colony of heaven. As these Philippians walked the Macedonian streets they remembered that they were citizens of heaven and heaven's Sovereign was walking with them.

Think what this could mean today! It could transform our entire viewpoint of life. It could make the weak strong, the discouraged brave and the defeated victorious. It has the power of a new life for the purpose of Jesus Christ in life is the purpose of transformation.

The fact of the Lord's spiritual presence in our midst at the moment and the further promise of His imminent personal presence brings into view three things of personal importance to anyone desiring peace.

1. The Lord in the Midst. Verse 1.

"Therefore, my brethren dearly beloved and longed for, my joy and crown, so stand fast in the Lord, my dearly beloved."

This is the secret of security.

We are to "stand fast in the Lord." Personal peace is to be found in the security of Christ's presence. It is not the magic of a moment. It is not the result of ejaculated prayers. It is the result of daily growth through a life lived in Christ's presence. It is found in the strengthening elements of daily fellowship with Christ, meditation, prayer, faith and obedience.

To "stand fast" does not mean to stand still. We are to experience the unrest of a progressive holiness that puts life on the march. We are to move on with an ever-advancing life. True happiness, it is said, consists of "something to do, something to love and something to hope for." It is progressive and not recessive. It is forward looking. It is found in going on to the constantly approaching and constantly receding horizons of Christian experience.

2. The Lord in the Mind. Verses 2, 3.

"I beseech Euodias, and beseech Syntyche, that they be of the same mind in the Lord. And I intreat thee also, true yokefellow, help those women which laboured with me in the gospel, with Clement also, and with other my fellow-labourers, whose names are in the book of life."

This is the secret of unity.

Perhaps an incipient dissension was brewing in the church at Philippi among two women of distinction, Euodias and Syntyche. The remedy for this and all dissension and the secret of Christian unity is found in a mind like Christ's. The cause of the difficulty is not stated. But if it is true to form it was too small to mention. How grave small matters may become we have only to look around us in the church. These things would never mature to threaten the peace of the church unless we allowed them. The remedy is always found in our nearness to the Lord. The closer we are to Him the less room there will be for dissension. Sheath the tongue, tame the temper, stable the anger and get into orderly rank as the redeemed march on with a united front to face a common enemy and complete a commissioned task.

The principals in this incipient dissension were apparently women of distinction. But they who had helped were also hindering and in this case perhaps their hindering could become greater than their helping.

The tribute paid to these women is not only a recognition of their distinguished service to the church at Philippi, but an anticipation of the heroic service of Christian women through all the ages. But for women, many churches would have to be disbanded. In finance, in prayer, in attendance, in song, in teaching, in witness and in over-all faithfulness women have rendered Christ and the Church an incalculable service. They have stepped in when men have failed the Church by default. They have carried on when men have given up. They have established a measure of devotion and consecration seldom reached by men. Theirs is the major spiritual service in both church and home. They outstrip their distaff companions in zeal and faithfulness. If it were not for women the mission outposts would be stubbornly adhering to positions that are secondary and trivial.

Dissension, while often a mark of carnal contention, is not necessarily an evidence of Christianity's failure. It has been observed that "Christianity must be of divine origin for it lives in spite of its adherents." We limit the effectiveness of God's power through our carnal living but we do not destroy the value of God's truth. There is a resilience in the character of the gospel that makes it outlive the defects of its adherents and proponents.

The remedy for the threatened disunity is expressed in the words, "Be of the same mind in the Lord." This would not mean identical thought patterns. It would not mean thinking alike on all issues. With different people there would be diversified thought but all this diversity of thought could be brought into focus by being "of the same mind in the Lord." The Lord would be like the lens of a camera and when we recognized our oneness in Him it would focus thought through Him. Our vital union in Christ would soften and rub out the sharp and harsh lines of difference and unite in thought and affection. This indeed is the secret of Christian unity.

Beside the aforementioned women and Clement who was apparently a teacher in Philippi, the entreaty to unity is addressed to one who is called a "true yokefellow" and to one unidentified group whom he calls "other my fellowlabourers, whose names are in the book of life." This word "yoke-fellow" or fellow-in-yoke would seem to be a proper name, actually *Syzygus*. And it refers to someone of intimate acquaintance with Paul with whom he enjoyed the figurative conception of animals-in-yoke, working side by side in the field or on the threshing floor. Syzygus was strongly intreated to maintain unity in the Philippian church. Harmony in labor and unity in relationship are necessary parts of Christian life.

There are others in Philippi whom Paul does not address by name but simply calls them "my fellowlabourers." Here are people with a higher honor than comes by earthly identification and listing. They are found in the eternal Who's Who of heaven, "the book of life." So great and honorable are they in God's sight that their names are recorded in His book as future and irrevocable partakers of everlasting life. To be unknown to and unlisted in earth's registers is no loss at all if we are to be found in God's "book of life." A name here links one with divine certainty. It places us in relation to two worlds so we can reap the best benefits of both. It is honor unspeakable.

3. The Lord in the Heart. Verse 4.

"Rejoice in the Lord alway: and again I say, Rejoice."

This is the secret of tranquility.

Here is a double emphasis to rejoice. We are to make God the ground of our tranquility and gratitude. Peace is not produced by fluctuating fortunes or changing circumstances, hence we are urged to "rejoice in the Lord." There are times when we cannot rejoice in our circumstances. In such times "rejoice in the Lord." There are times when we cannot rejoice in the state of our health, or have satisfaction with ourselves or be content with our economic condition. In such moments "rejoice in the Lord." The possession of God as an abiding presence overrules every other factor in life. It is the cause of rejoicing.

Russell Conwell who built and maintained a university on the proceeds of his lecture, Acres of Diamonds, once made a study of the lives of several thousand millionaires. Some of these he found to be happy. But none of those who were happy were so because they had money. Dr. Conwell said, "Get money: get all you can. Get fame: get all you honestly can; but do not be deluded to believe that either money or fame, in themselves, will bring happiness." We are to find, instead, that the abiding and unchanging source of life's satisfactions are in God for man is a creature made for God and he cannot be what he was meant to be without the fulfillment of these intentions.

II. PEACE AND ITS RELATION TO PRAYER. Verses 5-7.

"Let your moderation be known unto all men. The Lord is at hand. Be careful for nothing; but in every thing by prayer and supplication with thanksgiving let your requests be made known unto God. And the peace of God, which passeth all understanding, shall keep your hearts and minds through Christ Jesus."

Peace has a direct and immediate relation to God. The only known spiritual agencies which provide such an immediate relation to God is prayer.

Peace is not something objective for which a person is to make a search, for he who goes out to find peace as the object of search will never find it.

Peace is not a set of circumstances into which we may be brought and in which we may live without change and disturbance. Change is a mark of life. We are constantly faced with one problem after another and peace and satisfaction come in their solving. "The continuous encounter with continually changing conditions is the very substance of living." Peace, therefore, is not something we search for. It is not a set of perfect circumstances. It is the by-product of other factors. In the previous case it was "in the Lord." In this case it is in prayer. In other cases it is in truth, service and conquest. But always it is related to God in the life. The beginning of peace is to begin with Jesus Christ. This is sensible and reasonable for unrest and distress have their cause in deficient human character. This deficiency is congenital and goes back to man's alienation from God. Any correction must be at the point of this alienation and since Jesus Christ is God's only known remedy for our entire racial problem and individual character problem, it means that the personal beginning of peace is with Him.

We find that two conditions, one having to do with our human relationships and the other having to do with our divine relationships, determine the possession of peace in any situation.

1. The First Condition. Verse 5.

"Let your moderation be known unto all men."

Here is the man-ward aspect of peace. It is the result of our human relationships. In this sense it is the effect of good public relations. The word given to govern these relations is "moderation." It lends itself to a number of related meanings such as pliability, agreeableness, forbearance or sweet reasonableness. It is the spirit of life and attitude to others that forbears under injuries, does not desire revenge, is ready to forgive, possesses a gentleness of temper, and is moderate and temperate in physical desires.

Peace comes when we avoid extremes. The extremes of emotion develop explosive tempers and explosive tempers can only result in bad public relations. The extremes of will result in stubbornness and this will create antagonism. The extremes of desire breed greed and discontent and there will be no peace where there is an inordinate desire for material things or an intemperate spending of substance. "Some men are as covetous as if they were to live forever: and others are as prodigal as if they were to die the next moment." Peace and satisfaction come neither to the stingy nor the spendthrift. A good rule to follow is to "never allow your yearnings to exceed your earnings."

There are also to be considered the extremes of opinion. This appeal to moderation as the first condition of peace may have a contextual reference to the personality difficulties current at Philippi. It may have been an unwillingness to yield previous positions. We can afford to yield points but not principles. God cannot enjoy those who know so much that all knowledge rests with them. They remind us of what Job said to his critics: "no doubt but ye are the people, and wisdom shall die with you." These people menace the peace of our Christian communities. They push stubbornly on in arrogant self-esteem. To make one's way through a crowd demands pliability and yieldedness. One does not become so rude as to demand that everyone move out of his way. He side-steps first to the left and then to the right and achieves progress with goodwill.

I can recall being taken on a holiday as a small boy. We went by overnight steamer from Chicago to Saugatuck, Michigan. The last few miles of the journey required the navigation of the circuitous Saugatuck River. As I stood near the wheelhouse I watched the pilot as he spun the wheel first to one quarter of the compass and then the other. He was exercising the good sense of pliability. He yielded a point to one side and then to the other side. He recognized his circumstances and if he could not fly straight over the hills as a bird, he would get there by ship through the moderation of good navigation. It is in some such similar manner as this that we must go through life, observing good public relations by recognizing that life is sometimes a circuitous and devious course. It is not always straight ahead but has many bends and turns and we must yield to the presence of others and recognize the course of circumstances.

Peace and happiness do not depend on position so much as disposition.

2. The Second Condition. Verse 6.

"Let your requests be made known unto God."

This is the God-ward aspect of peace. In the

previous case it was our relationship with our fel-lowman where *moderation* was the key to good public relations. In this case it is our relationship with God where *prayer* is the key to peace. The combined result of pliability and prayer will be peace.

What kind of prayer-life brings peace? Paul states it in these words, "Be careful for nothing; but in every thing by prayer and supplication with thanksgiving let your requests be made known unto God." This is Arthur S. Way's translation: "Let no anxieties fret you: in every matter let the things you would ask be made known by means of prayer —by definite requests—linked with thanksgiving, at God's throne. And so the peace that God gives, the peace that transcends all conception, shall be the fortress-warder of your hearts, of all your thought, in this your life in Messiah Jesus."

A familiar treatment of this Scripture puts it this way: "Be careful for nothing: be thankful for anything: be prayerful in everything."

The elements of a peace-producing prayer life are as follows:

(1) Prayer that begins without excessive care. *"Be careful for nothing."*

In modern English this would read—"in nothing be anxious." Careful means anxious or worried. It is an unworried concern which we are to have in all things. Worry is the unrest we pay for the unbelief with which we mortgage life. Worry strangles the life of faith. Worry prevents the tranquility of spirit. Worry is the thief of a happy life.

To be without anxiety does not mean the lack of thoughtfulness or reasonable concern. It means being cautious without being fretfully anxious.

To be without care does not mean being indifferent to our circumstances. Instead it means to be concerned about God in those circumstances. With our eyes off of our anxieties and upon God we will have them off the source of distress and upon the secret of peace. After all peace does not come from what happens or does not happen around us. It is both a quality of character and an attitude to God.

How do we know when our care is excessive?

First, when we are more anxious about what we desire than about God's will. We never have peace by getting what we desire. Peace is found in God's will, with or without the things we think we need.

Second, when we are hurried into hasty and ill-advised action. He who prays can afford to wait because he is in relation to the God with whom there are no mistakes. Time is not an element with the God whose dimensions are eternity. It was Isaiah who said, "he that believeth shall not make haste" (Isa. 28:16).

Third, when we are constantly agitated in unrest. Unrest is not a characteristic of faith. It results in worry and worry is a breach of faith.

Worry never brings answers to prayer. It is faith which results in answered prayer and faith is trust without anxiety.

The neuroses which plague so many in this fast-moving day are not always caused by being worried over many things. Mental disease and nervous disorder come more often as the result of concentrated and continuous worry over one thing.

We are told to "be careful for nothing" which seems to be either presumptuous or ridiculous. How can one faced with real troubles and problems be without care for his adversity? Should we ignore them? There is as much danger in belittling our troubles as there is in magnifying them. It would indeed be presumptuous and foolish to do this. It does not say here, "Be careful for nothing" and stop. It says, "Be careful for nothing; but . . ." We are told to bring God into our life situations. It is not only to be careful but prayerful. Bringing God into the problem by means of prayer is neither ignoring the problem nor abandoning our own responsibilities. It is a recognition of the partnership of life into which salvation has brought us.

What kind of prayer brings peace?

(2) Prayer that prays for everything—*"in every thing by prayer and supplication."*

Nothing is excluded either from the need or the aid of prayer. Its necessity is only exceeded by its efficiency. There is an all-encompassing invitation to prayer in the word "everything." It brings us to the secret of peace when our cares are turned into prayers.

It is to be "by prayer *and* supplication." This is not an overplay on words. Prayer is one thing and supplication another. *Prayer* is general devotion and includes worship and adoration. *Supplication* is personal and refers to that desperate, business-end of one's prayer life where his prayers are specific and intense.

> "Remember well in times of stress,
>   When you would all desires express,
>   That God still answers prayer.
>   For men in prayer to Him have turned
>   Throughout all ages, and have yearned
>   For Him, and found themselves ne'er spurned;
>   They found He answered prayer.
>   No prayer can e'er ascend in vain—
>   He gives His best, then gives again,
>   For God still answers prayer.
>   We often fail to comprehend
>   The things of God, our truest Friend,
>   But of His goods there is no end,
>   For still He answers prayer."

What kind of prayer brings peace?

(3) Prayer that is thankful—*"with thanksgiving."*

We are to be praiseful as well as prayerful.

Thanksgiving in the form of praise through prayer would indicate the suppliant's surrender to the will of God. It would be the opposite of anxiety and worry. Praise and thanksgiving is sound spiritual strategy in the pursuit of peace. It is a recognition that the majority of experiences is on the credit side of life. It is in the counting of them that we will see what God hath done. It is furthermore the creation of a happy heart for the reception and retention of coming blessings. Faith does not flourish in the spirit of gloom and pessimism. If a life full of care is filled with prayer, and if that prayer is filled with praise, it will result in peace. Peace is born and nourished by prayer.

What kind of prayer brings peace?

(4) Prayer that is specific—*"let your requests be made known unto God."*

Prayer is a particular exercise with a specific objective. It has both a subject and an object. In this case the subject concerns specific things to be prayed about while the object is peace.

We have to make our requests known—not to give God information for His sake. We should pray as if God needed it, for this will serve to emphasize the need of faith and will also prepare us for the answer of God.

Requests are to be made known "to God." Prayer is not a psychological exercise which has its only effect upon the one who prays. It recognizes God's management of life and His providential place in our lives. Prayer will have the double effect of producing a life *without earthly anxiety* for it is "being careful for nothing." It also produces a life with *heavenly familiarity* for it is "in everything" that we let our "requests be made known unto God."

3. The Result. Verse 7.

"And the peace of God, which passeth all understanding, shall keep your hearts and minds through
Christ Jesus."

We remember now the two conditions which
produce this result: First—"*let your moderation* be
made known unto all men." Second—"*let your requests be* made known unto *God.*" The result of
observing these conditions will be peace.

Peace is not the result of chance but choice. It
is not a matter of good luck or fortune. It is as definitely related to certain spiritual laws and conditions as health of body is related to certain physical
laws.

We notice three things about this peace.

(1) It is the "peace *of God.*"

It does not spring from the mind. It is not a
psychological effect. It does not come from events
outside us. Its source is God.

This "peace of God" is to be distinguished from
the *peace of reconciliation* spoken of in Romans 5:1
and which is a divinely produced moral feeling resulting from forgiveness and divine mercy. To let
our "moderation be made known unto all men"
brings the *peace of conciliation.* To let our "requests be made known unto God" brings the *peace
of intercession.* This is peace of soul which tranquil-
izes all the factors of personality into the stabilized
posture of contentment.

"The celebrated Austrian composer, Haydn, was in company with other distinguished persons. The conversation turned on the best means of restoring their mental energies, when exhausted with long and difficult studies. One said he had recourse, in such a case, to a bottle of wine—another that he went into company. Haydn, being asked what he would do, or did do, said that he retired to his closet and engaged in prayer—that nothing exerted on his mind a more happy and efficacious influence than prayer."

(2) It is peace *"which passeth all understanding."*

This peace is so wonderful and transcendant in nature, so unusual in its charm and praise, so satisfying in its effect that it exceeds the power of human thought to understand. But one does not need to analyze peace in order to enjoy it. The sunrise and sunset have beautiful colors. There are reasons for these phenomena. And while it is good to know these reasons, such as the refraction of light, it does not add to the beauty of their coloring to know why they are so beautiful. It is so with God's peace which is beyond the reach of the mind but within the reach of Christian experience.

(3) It is peace which "keeps."

How unlike human peace is this "peace of God" which, it is promised, "shall keep your hearts and minds through Christ Jesus." Here is a military term used by Paul because the Philippians would understand military terminology since Philippi as a Roman colony contained a garrison of soldiers which guarded and defended its citizens. "Shall keep" actually means to "mount guard" or stand sentry. And in similar fashion the "peace of God" is like God's sentry which mounts guard and patrols the gates of the mind and the outposts of the heart. It stands in faithful and protective service at the gateway of our thinking to keep out worry and any other enemy. It holds the fort at the gateway of our feelings to act against any threatened intrusion and disturbance.

The usual human search for peace is an effort in which men fervently try to keep peaceful But peace is not a feeling to be kept. It is a quality of inward life which keeps us. It is this nature of God's peace which so clearly distinguishes it from the peace by books. Here is the establishment of a rapport with God that makes peace the fortress-warder of the soul and puts it on guard against all the alien elements of a disturbing and distracting world.

The possession of this peace does not mean our removal from a world of reality or escape from the struggles of life. It does not mean exemption from life's troubles and difficulties. It does not mean retreat from responsibility. It does mean that within the soul of its possessor is an inviolate citadel founded in righteousness, maintained by purity, sustained by prayer and equipped with faith. At the door of this citadel stands "the peace of God" to turn back rebellious and destructive enemies.

"FEAR NOT, O child of God, e'en though the way
    Be dark, and foes abound on every side;
    The Lord thy God is with thee day by day,
    He never will forsake, whate'er betide.
FRET NOT, O child of God, though troubles roll
Across thy path, and fright thee sore;
    The Lord thy God will guide thy soul,
    His angels will defend thee evermore.
FAIL NOT, O child of God, though Satan's host
May fierce assail, and strive to drag thee down;
    The Christ will save unto the uttermost.
    And thou shalt have at last a starry crown.
FAINT NOT, O child of God, e'en though the fight
Shall press thee sore, and drain thy strength;
    Though faint, press on, and soon will pass the night;
FORGET NOT, child of God, His wondrous love;
    Think oft upon His mercy and His grace,
    'Till thou shalt reach thy home above,
    And look forevermore upon His face."

III. PEACE AND ITS RELATION TO THE MIND.
Verses 8, 9.

"Finally, brethren, whatsoever things are true, whatsoever things are honest, whatsoever things are just, whatsoever things are pure, whatsoever things are lovely, whatsoever things are of good report; if there be any virtue, and if there be any praise, think on these things. Those things, which ye have both learned, and received, and heard, and seen in me, do: and the God of peace shall be with you."

We come to the second "finally" in this epistle. The first was in 3:1 where the apostle says, "Finally, my brethren, rejoice." Here he says, "Finally, brethren . . . think."

In this textual vicinity are to be found in proper proximity and precise order three important functions of Christian experience. In verse 6 it is *praying*—this is intercession. In verse 8 it is *thinking*—this is meditation. In verse 9 it is *doing*— this is action. Someone has said, "What we say on our knees is of less importance than what we do when we rise." This is only partially true. It might be better put if we said, what we do when we rise from our knees is as important as what we say while on our knees. Prayer is the normal prelude to action.

Deeds are the fruit of a normal Christian life. Thoughts are the seeds which produce these deeds. Prayer is the soil in which these seeds germinate and spring to action. All three must be found in our experience if we are to live a normal spiritual life.

In the gardens of the Rodin Museum in Paris stands the artist's statue of The Thinker. It is the picture in stone of a young man sitting on a large boulder. One arm lies across a knee. The chin rests on the upturned hand of the other arm and with the wrinkled brow the posture gives the evident impression of deep thought. But this is not the picture of the Christian thinker. He is to be better seen with one knee in the posture of prayer. The other knee which is just risen from prayer is in a forward position as if the thinker is about to rise for action; while the hand is extended in anticipated service and aid to whoever needs it. Thus the Christian comes from the presence of God to engage in thinking God's thoughts after Him while preparing himself for action in service.

We consider now two of these three important functions of Christian experience, namely, thinking and doing.

1. Thinking. Verse 8.

> "Finally, brethren, whatsoever things are true, whatsoever things are honest, whatsoever things are just, whatsoever things are pure, whatsoever things are lovely, whatsoever things are of good report; if there be any virture, and if there be any praise, think on these things."

The frustrations of great minds which continually omit God is illustrated in a statement by the late George Bernard Shaw. "There are two tragedies in life—one is not to get your heart's desire. The other is to get it." Imagine a squirrel cage existence in which one could never reach the legitimate objective of attaining his heart's desire or constantly sitting on either horn of a dilemma in which one was just as intolerable as the other. This frustration comes from the lack of that fundamental wisdom which the Bible states thus; "The fear of the Lord is the beginning of wisdom."

The Bible advocates a form of thought-control: not, of course, that control which is the technique of intolerance and dictators, for this thought control is in the form of positive thinking that gives the largest possible liberty to life. A modern psychologist who promises to fix up any patient in six easy lessons for a price of $1000, says, "the happy person does not waste time thinking. Self control comes from no control at all." Here is folly at its peak performance. It is liberalism run wild. Imagine an uninhibited mind without restraints and checks or without the channel of a deep and satisfying thought life such as we are offered here.

What is thinking? Is it "putting salt on the tail of an idea?" Only metaphorically. It is more. For the Christian it is an engagement with God and a preparation for life. It is to "think God's thoughts after Him." It is to sweep the vast horizon of deity and then come down to the reality of man's world of need with the proper understanding for life and action.

A properly directed and controlled thought life is important for two reasons:

(1) *Because what we think we become.*

If we analyzed our thinking habits we would be surprised at their content, their shallowness and their direction. It would reveal a pattern of market-thinking, money-thinking, pleasure-thinking, self-thinking and scandal—thinking. Seldom do the ennobling thoughts suggested here make up the ingredients of our thought life. We must not then be

176 Philippians: Where Life Advances

surprised at the end-product they produce in the persons we are.

It is still true that "as [a man] thinketh in his heart, so is he." We are not what we think we are but what we think, we are. "Our character takes on the complexion of our thoughts. If a man is cherishing noble thoughts he cannot help becoming noble; if he is generous in his thoughts, he will be likewise in his acts; if he is loving and tender in his thoughts, he will be also in his acts." Our minds are the looms in the wonderful machinery of the inner life. Our thoughts are the threads which weave the garments our souls will wear. If you care for your thoughts you will wear worthy garments on your soul.

There is no quicker way to deteriorate and degenerate than to fill the mind with unworthy thoughts. Witness the tragedy referred to in the first chapter of Romans where men refused to retain God in their thoughts and gave themselves up to vile and ungodly thinking. They became ultimately consumed and destroyed by vile affections and degenerated beyond description.

"Failures are divided into two classes—those who thought and never did, and those who did and never thought."

Bishop Lubbock spoke of the prejudiced thinking of some people—"Sometimes we think we think when all we are doing is rearranging our prejudices." It is said of some people that their minds are like concrete, all mixed up and permanently set.

Along the Lackawanna Railroad some years ago they painted the word "think" to stimulate efficiency, safety and pleasure in railroading. This word was painted on the buttresses of bridges, the sides of loading platforms, the doors of section houses and the walls of buildings. Who can measure the effect of such a campaign on the minds of workers? Who could measure it in our everyday lives if we placed it in conspicuous places in our life? No doubt it would transform our existence. "Finally brethren . . . think."

(2) *Because our thoughts are the channel of the transforming Grace of God.*

God's grace in its transforming work operates through our thought-life and not through emotions or imaginations. Thought may be stimulated by emotion but transformation is through the mind. This does not mean the superficial thing some think it to mean. It is not simply to think of lovely things. More is needed. We need a monitor for our minds. We need the presence of divine grace, using the thought-life as its instrument of transformation.

Jesus said, "A good man out of the good treasure of his heart bringeth forth that which is good; and an evil man out of the evil treasure of his heart bringeth forth that which is evil: for of the abundance of the heart his mouth speaketh" (Luke 6:45). In terms of psychology this treasure is the subconscious mind. What the conscious mind dwells upon in its thinking gradually sinks into this hidden treasury and becomes the material for character, memory and action. It is upon this unconscious part of our being that the Holy Spirit works in the transforming of character and life. It is important then that the substance of our thinking be such that this subconscious treasury be stored with the precious elements of truth and nobility.

He who thinks God's thoughts after Him will become godlike. But if we allow thoughts of selfishness, anger, covetousness, discontent, hatred, jealousy and lust to occupy the mind we become partaker of their nature. If we are what we eat it is much more true that we are what we think.

The components of the Bible become the elements of a complete education. Someone has stated it this way: "Get all the education you can. Master as much of the intensive fields of knowledge as possible, but with all your getting, get wisdom. Remember always that the fear of the Lord is the beginning of wisdom. Know history, and experience the history of redemption. Study geography, and learn the way to the River of Life and the City whose Builder and Maker is God. Study geology, and plant your feet upon the Rock of Ages. Study zoology, and bow in reverence before the majesty of the Lion of the tribe of Judah. Study biology, and begin now the Life Eternal. Study botany, and yield your soul to the sweet influence of its

Rose of Sharon and Lily of the Valley. Study astronomy, and follow the gleam of your soul's Bright and Morning Star that has risen with healing in His beams. Study psychology, and sit at the feet of Him who knew what was in man. Study law, and light your torch in the flame that burned on Mount Sinai. Study medicine, and keep en rapport with the Great Physician. Study business administration, and be fervent in spirit, serving the Lord. Study art, and practice the art of fine living. Study philosophy, and remember always that the highest philosophy is the formula of a perfect life."

Here are the six things which comprise a proper Christian thought-life.

(a) Whatsoever Things are TRUE.

This must underlie everything which is intended to be right whether it is a building, a battleship or a life. Life can never be right if our thinking is wrong. True thinking is truth in doctrine, faith and practice.

Many need a revised version of their thoughts because they are in some cases unethical and untrue and in others prejudiced and biased. Some are like religious tumbleweeds, "tossed to and fro, and carried about with every wind of doctrine."

Shakespeare said, "If thou wilt to thyself be true thou canst not be false to any man." This is a standard of action that is as Scriptural as it is true because our attitudes to others are a response to our own inner selves.

(b) Whatsoever Things are HONEST.

Dishonesty is one of the most withering blights of human character. It is the carnal willingness to lie. In court, lying is perjury and the very bulwarks of society are undermined by the frequency of perjured testimony. It appears in the misrepresentations of advertising. It is found in the immoralities of society. And at this moment it may be gnawing at the vitals of our own character. Let us think honestly and we will speak and act with honesty.

(c) Whatsoever Things are JUST.

This is the justice and fairness with which we are to treat our fellowman. The mind becomes the scales of justice that weighs and considers the case before judgment is passed. It does not allow one bad thing to outweigh the preponderance of good things. It is the care we exercise against taking everything for granted. It is refusing to make a fact out of a rumor. Some years ago a popular prose-poem went the rounds which was titled, "Rumoresque."

> "A gray-haired stranger in a cart rode through our town, he drove a dumpy, pony mare, his clothes were faded brown. He asked the road to Seven Springs; three of us heard him say that he would thank us kindly to be shown the nearest way. He got his information, appreciation showed, bespoke a pleasant evening, and jogged upon his road.

"Now this was positively all; we saw the man no more but one there was who saw him pass before her open door. And, phoning to a friend, she told how this peculiar man had driven by as if he led a monster caravan. The other soon, phone-visiting, informed another friend about the weird procession that seemed to have no end.

"Ere long the phones were ringing from here to Seven Springs, and the women folks on every farm were hearing wondrous things. 'Tis said a circus had been wrecked upon the main railway, so it was moving overland to save a great delay. The caravan was two miles long, and nearly every night some hungry animal got loose; the neighborhood took fright.

"They called the husbands from the fields, the children from the schools, got out the guns, chained up the gates, and hid the woodshed tools. The panic lasted for an hour, then dwindled quickly down, when someone got a message that no circus was in town. The huge parade had not been seen; on all the thoroughfares there was no sign of men and teams, no elephants or bears.

"Indignant then, the neighbors sought to find the guilty one who started such a fable out; it easily was done, for as each questioned each, they found that each one in her way had added just a bit to what she'd heard somebody say. So when the tale was sifted through, it shriveled down to where the gray-haired stranger jogged along behind his dumpy mare."

Scandal is defined as "something that has to be bad in order to be good." The mind that feasts on scandal will savour of a sewer.

"If there be those who spread false rumors,
    Think only of the true.
If some believe all men dishonest,
    Give honesty its due.
If scandal sullies life's white pages,
    Turn to the one still pure;
Man does not build on wrecks of others
    Those structures that endure.
If some folks take a sordid pleasure
    In raking mud and slime;
Consider flowers that spring from muckheaps
    Without a trace of grime.
Look for the virtue, not the baseness;
    Be quick to offer praise;
And peace of mind will be your portion,
    Rare friendships bless your days."
                —Anna M. Priestley

The mind has been set up by someone in the form of a store with the thinker cast in the role of the storekeeper who must determine whether his will be a just mind or a junk mind. He has a limited space to carry his goods which are thoughts. He must be careful in the selection of his mental merchandise. He can make a junk shop of the mind and let it be cluttered with bitterness, suspicion, jealousy, malice and hatred or he can stock up with noble ambitions, delightful friendships, useful information, inspiring thoughts, golden memories, worthwhile interests and priceless scriptures. Wise mental merchandising brings great profit in the business of living.

(d) Whatsoever Things are PURE.

Here is thought in the chaste and virgin nature of moral purity. There can be no purity of our members without purity of our minds. Jesus pointed out that the impure thinker was equal in culpability to the person of impure acts and life.

One of the greatest of modern disasters was the deluge created by the breaking of the St. Francis Dam in the Santa Clara watershed, forty-two miles north of Los Angeles. Without warning its foundations gave way in the middle of the night and the lives of at least 500 sleeping persons were snuffed out. A thundering cascade of swirling water, as high as 125 feet at its crest, roared its way through a narrow 65 mile path from the dam site to Montalvo, a little coastal town below Ventura. It swept relentlessly through Piru, Fillmore, Bardsdale and Santa Paula. The victims of this gigantic wall of floodwater were forewarned only by the noise of the onward mountain of angry water which up-rooted trees, lifted homes from their foundations, crushing boxcars, automobiles, farm buildings and sweeping livestock and poultry on to destruction. Built only two years before its collapse, St. Francis Dam had been declared to be the last word in engineering and the safest dam ever built. It was discovered that a portion of the dam was built on a faulty shale formation. Water seepage imperceptibly ate away at the foundation and so weakened its inner structure that the relentless pressure of 36,000 acre-feet of water forced it into collapse. This is the way men collapse morally. The inner thought life harbors the impure thought which destroys the moral defenses of the mind and when temptation comes there is no defense to meet it. Then there is collapse and destruction and another life has been swept into moral ruin. We must observe this rule—"Whatsoever things are pure."

(e) Whatsoever Things are LOVELY.

This means amiable and gracious—literally "loveable." The spiritual effect of grace is graciousness. Thoughts steeped in this atmosphere give a pleasant definition to our Christian character.

(f) Whatsoever Things are of GOOD REPORT.

This item concludes the double triad in our mental menu. It means in a proper sense that which is "high-toned." It is nothing snobbish but means to be elevated with an absence of bitterness and rancor. It is illustrated by the elders mentioned in the eleventh chapter of Hebrews who by their faith "obtained a good report." The best possible report that can come from our lives comes as a result of our thought-life which will inspire noble action.

There is another sense in which we may think of this quality of our thought-life. Good report is the opposite of bad and evil report or gossip. It is "out of the abundance of the heart [that] the mouth speaketh." There is a Chinese proverb which says, "Think twice and say nothing." Why not change it to think right and say something? We are not expected to be mental and vocal marionettes but our speech should "be alway with grace, seasoned with salt" (Col. 4:6).

What we say is an important part of the success and happiness of our lives. "It takes a baby approximately two years to learn to talk and between sixty and seventy years to learn to keep his mouth shut." This refers to the struggle for sound speech or that which is of good report.

Perhaps we can see here a warning against the evil practice of gossip which is so ruinous to our human relations. The word gossip is totally different now from its original meaning. It came from the Anglo-Saxon word "godsib" which meant "related to God." It was used of a sponsor at baptism thus indicating that a godsib was a friend who was familiar with you and knew all about you. Time has changed the word from the idea of knowing all about you to telling all about you with evil connotations. Gossip is a vicious exchange of ideas dealing largely in the currency of scandal and ignoring "whatsoever things are of good report."

To finalize the matter, here are six things that provide the mental staples and ingredients for a wholesome and holy thought-life. The challenge is, "Finally brethren . . . think."

2. Doing. Verse 9.

"Those things, which ye have both learned, and received, and heard, and seen in me, do: and the God of peace shall be with you."

"Finally brethren . . . think" is properly coun-
terbalanced by "these things . . . do." Thinking
and doing are parts of a whole. They are both
created in the atmosphere of prayer and thus linked
to and energized by God. What we are to think
is given in a list of thought principles. What we
are to do is seen in the apostle's life. Few, apart
from Christ, would dare such an utterance or stand
such a test.

Thought and action are the very life of the
Christian. He cannot properly exist apart from
these functions of experience which will produce
the greatest happiness and fruitfulness.

To "do" is to complete the triad of Christian
living as it is found in praying, thinking, and doing.
Praying and thinking can only be fulfilled in doing.
These are expressions that must result in experience.

The Christian life is not only a contemplative
exercise but one of action and accomplishment.
Thumb-rolling is not the index of true piety. It is
found in devotion and meditation that are followed
by a life of service and action. Jesus said, "If ye
know these things, happy are ye if ye do them."

What is the result of such holy action? It is
that "the God of peace shall be with you." In verse
7 it was the "peace of God." Here the God who
works this peace and mediates it to us through
prayer manifests Himself to us as the person producing peace. And the God of this peace reveals
Himself in the life which not only prays but thinks

and acts in consonance with the revelation of Himself in His Word.

IV. PEACE AND ITS RELATION TO OUR CIRCUMSTANCES Verses 10-19.

"But I rejoiced in the Lord greatly, that now at the last your care of me hath flourished again; wherein ye were also careful, but ye lacked opportunity. Not that I speak in respect of want: for I have learned, in whatsoever state I am, therewith to be content. I know both how to be abased, and I know how to abound: every where and in all things I am instructed both to be full and to be hungry, both to abound and to suffer need. I can do all things through Christ which strengtheneth me. Notwithstanding ye have well done, that ye did communicate with my affliction. Now ye Philippians know also, that in the beginning of the gospel, when I departed from Macedonia, no church communicated with me as concerning giving and receiving, but ye only. For even in Thessalonica ye sent once and again unto my necessity. Not because I desire a gift: but I desire fruit that may abound to your account. But I have all, and abound: I am full, having received of Epaphroditus the things which were sent from you, an odour of a sweet smell, a sacrifice acceptable, well pleasing to God. But my God shall supply all your need according to his riches in glory by Christ Jesus."

Our circumstances do not produce peace but an inner peace is a big factor in our attitude to our circumstances. It is also true that a greater state of peacefulness will result from the stabilization that comes to life in the various areas of experience. This section of the epistle covers three areas of experience, and sets forth three great sufficiencies.

1. How to Be Satisfied Wherever You Are.
   Verses 10-12.

"But I rejoiced in the Lord greatly, that now at the last your care of me hath flourished again; wherein ye were also careful, but ye lacked opportunity. Not that I speak in respect of want: for I have learned, in whatsoever state I am, therewith to be content. I know both how to be abased, and I know how to abound: everywhere and in all things I am instructed both to be full and to be hungry, both to abound and to suffer need."

This is contentment in *all circumstances.*

It is easy to define contentment but difficult to find it. It is usually so because we seek contentment in the possession and the abundance of things. We assume that we will be content if we could have different circumstances or a better place in life. We crave a certain honor or a higher salary thinking that contentment will accompany advancement or enrichment. But we discover that it is an elusive thing, always just out of reach of each advancing step.

Contentment does not depend on *what* you have or *where* you are but *who* you are.

Contentment is not an economic quality but a spiritual attainment. A tub was large enough for Diogenes but the whole world was too small for Alexander.

Contentment is not a state of account but a state of heart. It comes to those who find it within rather than without. In the pursuit to find contentment in what is without we discover "the land of promise is always more extensive than the land of possession."

Contentment is found in making the most of the least. If your portion is pain, make the most and best of it. If your portion is limited circumstances, make the most of them. If, however, your portion is plenty and pleasure, make the most of them and do not take them for granted.

Paul had previously expressed his discontent with himself. He was dissatisfied with his personal progress and record. This is right. This is spiritual reality. But contentment through one's spiritual attainment is possible and desirable, and it is this attainment Paul reaches here.

I was conversing with a friend of mine one day when the subject of conversation drifted to our respective sons and their careers. My friend remarked concerning his boy that "he had not yet reached his angle of repose." Upon inquiry it was explained that every object has its own angle of repose. It is that angle at which the object is in a state of equilibrium. When we can say, "I have learned in whatsoever state I am, therewith to be content," we have reached our angle of repose, our state of equilibrium and rest.

Paul uses two educational terms to describe his experience. It is not a gift handed to us but a lesson learned in the school of life.

(1) *"I have learned."* Verse 11.

Paul did not receive contentment out of a theory in an academic classroom. It was in the school of life, at Jerusalem, in Arabia, at Lystra, Derbe, Antioch and Ephesus. Now he was at Rome and here there was a difference in his attitude because he had learned his lessons well. And we remember that he wrote of this contentment from the confinement of prison in Rome. It was not Paul's Sunday language that changed with his Monday experience.

(2) *"I am instructed."* Verse 12.

Paul had known the separated extremes of experience in being abased in one instance and abounding in another. He knew fullness and emptiness. He had experienced pain and pleasure. It was common in Paul's day to speak of rivers running low and being abased. Then when they ran at flood tide from bank to bank they abounded. Paul knew life in these extremes. He knew it when it ran low and its resources were a bare trickle over its pebbly bed. He knew it when it was running high and running over and everything looked promising. He knew it in the comfort of the home of

Priscilla and Aquila at Corinth, but also in the austerities and deprivations of the prison at Rome. He knew it in plenty and poverty, sickness and health, joy and sorrow, weakness and strength, evil report and good report. But in all these extremes he "was instructed" in the art of contentment.

There is a parable of contentment about a violet which shed its modest beauties at the turfy foot of an old oak. It lived there many days during the kind summer in obscurity. The winds and the rains came and fell, but they did not hurt the violet. Storms often crashed among the boughs of the oak. And one day the oak said, "Are you not ashamed of yourself when you look up at me, you little thing down there, when you see how large I am, and how small you are; when you see how small a space you fill, and how widely my branches are spread?" "No," said the violet, "we are both where God has placed us; and God has given us both something. He has given to you strength, to me sweetness; and I offer Him back my fragrance, and I am thankful." "Sweetness is all nonsense," said the oak; "a few days—a month at most—where and what will you be? You will die, and the place of your grave will not lift the ground higher by a blade of grass. I hope to stand some time—ages, perhaps— and then when I am cut down, I shall be a ship to bear men over the sea, or a coffin to hold the dust of a prince. What is your lot to mine?" "But," cheerfully breathed back the violet, "we are both what God made us, and we are both where He placed us. I suppose I shall die soon. I hope to die fragrantly, as I have lived fragrantly. You must be cut down at last; it does not matter, that I see, a few days or a few ages, my littleness, or your largeness, it comes to the same thing at last. We are what God made us. We are where God placed us. God gave you strength; God gave me sweetness."

You have heard people say that they were "sitting pretty." Experience tells us that we do not sit there for long because no state is static. There is constant change in life. Fortunes fluctuate and circumstances change. Life is a variable experience from abasing to abounding.

Contentment can come not just because we have conquered our circumstances but because we have learned to live with them. A man was justifiably proud of his lawn until one year a heavy crop of dandelions appeared. He tried everything he had ever heard of to get rid of them, but without success. At last he wrote to a school of agriculture, giving a list of the remedies he had tried, and ending with an appeal: "What shall I do now?" In due course he received this reply: "We suggest that you learn to love them."

It is not the intention of Scripture to suggest our contentment and pleasure with the *status quo*. Life must advance. It must progress. We must be better today than we were yesterday. The person who is content with his lot because he is lazy and unprogressive is not content with much. Let contentment be in the context of our pressing on "toward the mark for the prize of the high calling of God in Christ Jesus."

There are many substitute offers for the real thing. In many forms of pleasure and possession the world bids us be content but no substitute can achieve what the real contentment of the Bible offers us. The director of a radio show wanted to get the sound effect of water being poured out of a barrel onto some boards. They tried peas on oiled paper, but that wasn't it. They tried dropping pins on a taut square of silk, and that wasn't it. Finally, a quiet fellow who was standing by said, "Suppose you try pouring water out of a barrel onto some boards." They did; and that was it.

2. How to Be Strong for Whatever You Must Do. Verse 13.

"I can do all things through Christ which strengtheneth me."

This is strength for *all things* as in verses 11 and 12 it was contentment in *all circumstances.*

All of us have faced situations which were too much for us and we failed. But no situation is too much for Jesus Christ. If we had brought His power into our weakness we could have succeeded. The normal Christian life is a victorious one.

When we live normally we are living in the experience of this verse where we have strength for all things. The principle expressed here gives proper place to the regenerated personality of the Christian. It neither minimizes or magnifies that place. It does not tell us that the Christian does everything for himself. Nor does it teach that God does everything for the Christian, relieving him of responsibility and effort. What it does teach is that there is a place for the regenerated personality. God makes us responsible to "do" while He becomes responsible to supply us with the strength and power to do. It will be Christ's presence in our person and His power for our problem.

Instead of telling us that Christ does everything and we do nothing, it says, "I can do [everything] through Christ which strengtheneth me." I must do and He must enable me to do. I must act and He must enable me to act. I must speak and He must enable me to speak. I must work and He must enable me to work.

In the victorious life God uses the regenerated personality. He does not set it aside or ignore it or minimize it or even supplant it so that we simply become spiritual puppets for whom a higher power pulls the strings. Will power is an important factor in the victorious life. It can be described as our will plus God's power. We supply the will and God provides the power.

If the Christian life were an automatic response

to a divine stimulus, then all Christians would act alike and without variation. But since both the human will and the divine power are required, it accounts for a variety in Christian experience as well as various capacities in Christian service.

Such ability as this verse describes belongs to a full-orbed and well-rounded Christian experience. It is linked with a whole chapter of truth and a full variety of experiences. The experiences include all the normal possibilities in the Christian life. It includes the possibility to live steadfast (vs. 1); to live in moderation (vs. 5); to live without excessive care and worry (vs. 6); to live in peace (vs. 7); to live a consistent thought-life (vs. 8); to live a life of appropriate Christian action (vs. 9); to live a contented life (vs. 11); to live with adequate strength (vs. 13); to live with sufficient means for life (vs. 19).

In the face of duty and opportunity we can either plead impotence or claim omnipotence. The secret lies in Jesus Christ. His presence in us means His power for us. Then we can say, "I can do all things through Christ which strengtheneth me." Take this verse and reduce it to its four fundamental and qualifying words and you have life's simplest and most sufficient secret—"I can . . . through Christ."

What are some of the things that any Christian can do through Christ?

(1) *He can be "salt" and "light."*

Jesus said, "Ye are the salt of the earth . . . ye are the light of the world." We are salt to be a preventive and preservative. We are light to be illuminating. What we are in character we can be in conduct. Therefore be what you are.

(2) *He can be a witness.*

Jesus said, "Ye shall receive power . . . and ye shall be witness unto me" (Acts 1:8). What I have been sent to be I can be.

(3) *He can be fruitful.*

Jesus said, "Ye have not chosen me, but I have chosen you, and ordained you, that ye should go and bring forth fruit, and that your fruit should remain" (John 15:16). What I have been ordained to do I can do, for abiding means abounding.

(4) *He can maintain good works.*

"This is a faithful saying, and these things I will that thou affirm constantly, that they which have believed in God might be careful to maintain good works" (Titus 3:8). Since faith without works is dead I can maintain these things through His life for I work out what He works in.

(5) *He can live without habitual sin.*

"We know that whosoever is born of God sinneth not" (I John 5:18).

There is a difference between occasional sin and habitual sin. One may be unconsciously committing the one without consciously committing the other. The habit of life before regeneration was to sin. The habit of life after regeneration is to sin not. This is possible because "I can do all things through Christ which strengtheneth me." There are other things I can do. What I can do I ought to do. What I ought to do I must do.

A member of one of Arturo Toscanini's Philharmonic Symphony orchestras said: "Under Toscanini we play better than we know." This reach of better things is possible to those who live under the mastership of Jesus Christ. He is the Maestro of life. Under Him we can *live* better than we know.

    (3) How to Be Supplied with Whatever You Need. Verses 14-19.

> "Notwithstanding ye have well done, that ye did communicate with my affliction. Now ye Philippians know also, that in the beginning of the gospel, when I departed from Macedonia, no church communicated with me as concerning giving and receiving, but ye only. For even in Thessalonica ye sent once and again unto my necessity. Not because I desire a gift: but I desire fruit that may abound to your account. But I have all, and abound: I am full, having received of Epaphroditus the things which were sent from you, an odour of a sweet smell, a sacrifice acceptable, well pleasing to God. But my God shall supply all your need according to his riches in glory by Christ Jesus."

This is supply for *all needs* as in verses 11 and 12 it was contentment in *all circumstances* and in verse 13 it was strength for *all things*.

The promise of this sufficiency is in the words of verse 19, "But my God shall supply all your need according to his riches in glory by Christ Jesus." This promise is supported and made significant by the context which precedes it. In the area of these verses is to be found the proper understanding and appreciation of this provision.

We claim this familiar promise with more presumption than faith because we fail to note that it is predicated on a condition. We will never realize its replenishing provision until we fulfill its spiritual and circumstantial requirements. It is safe to say that every divine promise has its own condition of fulfillment.

What this promise proposes to do is to supply a need. Whatever created the need would determine how God would satisfy that need. We must have a legitimate need before we can have a legitimate claim on the divine supplier. In the case of the Philippians their need was created when they sent Epaphroditus to Rome with a gift. No doubt this gift was accumulated from the meagre necessities of life among the Philippian Christians. Therefore, because the Philippians had supplied Paul's need God would supply theirs. Their need was not created by extravagance, slothfulness, improvidence, unwillingness to work; or by over-ambitious and unwise investments; or by foolish and unnecessary spending. Whatever claims we have upon Philippians 4:19 must be legitimate. Its provision is not open to us merely because of desire, or because it is an easy way to live. The door of abundance is not opened to our whims. There is no magic by which we can command ourselves into a position of carefree ease. This is not an *open sesame* to slothful plenty. There is principle here.

God promises to meet human need for a purpose. That purpose is never to relieve us of responsibility. It is always because of responsibility to a higher law and motive. It is because of *previous giving* as in the case of the Philippians which created the need. Or it is because of God's knowledge of our *intended giving* as in the case of the Corinthians. "And God is able to make all grace abound toward you; that ye, always having all sufficiency in all things, may abound to every good work" (II Cor. 9:8). This Corinthian passage is the Bible's divine law of benevolence which promises the ability of means for those who dare to test the provision.

Dwight L. Moody said of this promise of verse 19 that was God's check. He conceived it as as follows:

"My God"—the name of the firm printed on the check.

"Shall supply"—the promise to pay.

"All your need"—the amount to be paid.

"His riches"—the deposit in the account against which the check is drawn.

"In glory"—the address of the bank.

"By Christ Jesus"—the signature which appears on the check.

This check needs but one thing to make it a practical and valuable thing—the endorsement of our faith on its reverse side.

A breakdown of this great promise-verse (vs. 19) will reveal some assuring things.

"My God." This reveals the proximity of God to our needs. He is more than a distant and impersonal Providence. He is our personal Heavenly Father. God is not confined to a heavenly splendor and limited by space and time. He is available in the midst of our need.

"Shall supply." This means to fufill. It could be reversed to say fill-full. God was going to fill-full what was wanting in the Philippians because of their benevolence to Paul.

"All your need." Here are no restrictions or limitations. The inclusive "all" embraces every need, physical, spiritual, mental, moral, financial and circumstantial. It includes guidance, strength, comfort, health, courage, food, employment and whatever else enters into human experience.

"According." The action of God in meeting the Philippians' needs will be accomplished by a divine ability that is measured by the abundance found in "riches in glory." And all of this abundance is related to the person of Jesus Christ. It is His riches in glory that is the guarantee of the supply of your need. And it is His personal presence in you that is the guarantee of God's knowledge of your need.

Some interesting items of Christian stewardship will yield to a closer examination of the incident which precedes this promise.

(1) *Christian courtesy.* Verses 10, 14, 16.

Here is the grace of thankfulness. Paul courteously and gratefully remembers to thank the Philippians. Courtesy is a too-oft neglected virtue. We must be quick to thank God and also those whom God has used.

(2) *The purpose behind giving.* Verse 17.

Whatever advantage Paul received by the gift was far exceeded in his estimation by the advantage that would accrue to the Philippians because of their gift.

Weymouth translates the passage as follows: "Not that I crave for gifts from you, but I do want to see a rich harvest of service placed to your account." Paul was not seeking gain for himself as his motives were devoid of all personal advantage. His interests were in the Philippians for whom he wanted a rich reward at the judgment. Whatever "account" is referred to here, it is not meant that God is keeping an account of credits and debits in relation to salvation. Salvation is not to be bargained for or worked for. There is a divine law of recompense which operates either for or against us —"He which soweth sparingly shall reap also sparingly; and he which soweth bountifully shall reap also bountifully."

(3) *Giving and receiving.* Verse 15.

The law of giving in the Bible is simple—"Give and it shall be given unto you." It is as simple as the law of harvest where we reap as we sow. Here those who have given will also receive. The faithful steward puts into effect inevitable forces which ultimately turn back upon the giver so that he becomes the receiver. Now the Philippians who, among all the churches, had been the most faithful givers were about to be the recipients of the divine supply as recorded in verse 19.

The fact that Philippi was a mission church reveals an example of benevolence and stewardship worthy of emulation. They were by no means affluent, yet out of their meagerness they gave abundantly. We sigh and say if we only had a lot of money we would give so much. That does not necessarily follow. It is not necessarily true that the possession of abundance would mean abundant giving. It is what we are now that determines what we will be. It is what we are giving now that determines what we will give later. It is not how much we have that constitutes the basis for giving, but our disposition to give of whatever means we may now possess. It is not what we would do with our thousands, but what we are doing with our tens and hundreds. The example was set by the Philippians and also by the Corinthians of whom

Paul spoke, "How that in a great trial of affliction the abundance of their joy and their deep poverty abounded unto the riches of their liberality" (II Cor. 8:2).

(4)   The gift to Paul was equivalent of a gift to God. Verse 18.

The form of the gift was physical but it passed through a metamorphosis in its character for it became "an odour of a sweet smell" unto God. How inspiring is that thought that a gift of love to someone in need, a sacrificial offering placed on the offering plate, is like the wafted scent of perfume to the spiritual sensibilities of God. In this sense giving means more than a gift. It involves the motive, spirit, faith, attitude and condition behind it.

This kind of giving was invested with the sacredness of Jewish sacrifices for it was regarded as a sacrificial offering to God. Thus stewardship is a sacred and holy exercise and not merely the incidental giving of an impersonal gift of money or charity. How differently we would give if we understood the nature of giving.

But it has to be a gift. A ticket for a church supper or a church bazaar, a purchase at a rummage sale, is not a gift; it is a financial transaction for which we have received a commodity of food or clothing in return. This is a depraved and disgraceful form of church finance which robs church giving of its significance. It prostitutes stewardship. It degrades ethics. It robs people of an inestimable privilege and God of the perfume of Christian devotion because it cannot become the "odour of a sweet smell" nor a "sacrifice acceptable, well pleasing" unto God. A return to basic New Testament stewardship would produce one of the greatest revivals of spiritual life ever known to the Church.

(5) The gift to Paul was an example of proper Christian relief. Verses 14, 16.

Christian relief and benevolence is properly personal benevolence rather than institutional benevolence. When we allow agencies to distribute our benevolence we lose the effect of personal contact with the need and the needy one. But essentially Christian relief is to be done through the church and not through government. The early church cared for its own so that it could be said, "Neither was there any among them that lacked."

It may be argued that times have changed and circumstances are different. The fact is still true that if the minimum of the tithe was observed as the voluntary principle and standard of stewardship, it would be sufficient to create a vast benevolent reservoir. This would be sufficient to build enough hospitals, clinics, orphanages, homes for the indigent and aged, means of rehabilitation as well as the maintenance to a point of luxury of every church and mission station of the world. Our churches are failing both God and man through their substandard stewardship. Christian steward-

ship would provide an adventure in living undreamed of by the average Christian.

To consider these three sufficiencies which
promise contentment in all circumstances (vss. 11,
12), strength for all things (vs. 13) and supply for
all needs (vs. 19) we observe Christianity facing
and meeting realities of our daily existence.

An old gentleman was watching a small boy
struggling with a very large apple. Finally he said
to the lad, "Too much apple, isn't it sonny?" The
little fellow with his mouth full of apple and his
hand full of more apple replied, "No sir, mister, not
enough boy." Our problem is not that there is too
much world, too much flesh, too much devil, too
much sin, too much temptation; but that there is
not enough Christianity. There is enough for us
but not enough in us. There is not enough reality
in our experience or appropriation by our faith to
provide us enough power to meet life's needs. Here
we find ourselves in the midst of "enough." There
is more than we will ever need or can ever use. Here
is enough Christianity for the emergency and the
regularity, for the contingency and the common-
place, for the monotonous and the momentous.

V. The Salutations of Farewell. Verses 20-23.

"Now unto God and our Father be glory for ever
and ever. Amen."

"Salute every saint in Christ Jesus. The brethren
which are with me greet you."

"All the saints salute you, chiefly they that are of Caesar's household."

"The grace of our Lord Jesus Christ be with you all. Amen."

Three words summarize the farewell: glory, greeting, grace. Glory "unto God" (vs. 20). Greeting unto "the saints" (vss. 21, 22). Grace unto "all" (vs. 23).

Sainthood is determined by one's relation to Jesus Christ. It is a nature received through the new birth. There were saints in Philippi and at Rome. These maintained the nature of their character in spite of the adversities of their place. They did not change their religious color, chameleon-like, according to their circumstances. Instead, their character changed their circumstances.

You will notice that in transmitting Christian greetings from the saints at Rome to the saints at Philippi Paul says, "chiefly they that are of Caesar's household." We know that at this time Rome was notoriously licentious and wicked. This was true both as a city and an empire. Since the seat of the empire was the city of Rome they had there the concentration of evil. The government was pagan and cruel. The rulers and courtiers were degraded and vicious. Yet in the midst of such conditions there was a noble company who were living to the glory of God. They were "of Caesar's household." It consisted of a vast company, not only in Rome but in such scattered colonies as Philippi. They belonged to every station of life such as courtiers, princes, servants, soldiers, secretaries, gardeners, teachers, artists, librarians, architects, economists, senators and slaves. There were also the members of the imperial family and relatives.

Only thirty years prior to Paul's incarceration in Rome, Christ had been crucified in a foreign country, a Roman province. Yet in these thirty years His influence had touched this imperial family and the government staff to such an extent and degree that Paul records the fact that many of them are now Christians. Here is an eloquent tribute to the power of the gospel. It vindicates the previous confidence of Paul who said when writing to the church at Rome, "I am not ashamed of the gospel of Christ: for it is the power of God unto salvation . . ." Here also is tribute to the versatility of the gospel. It is "indigenous to all climates, and will flourish in any soil." It is as possible to be a Christian in a royal court as in a slum, in a fashionable circle as amongst peasants and laborers, amongst rulers as amongst the poor and destitute."

Notice the last word of the Epistle—"The grace of our Lord Jesus Christ be with you all." This is characteristic of the entire book whose theme is centered in Christ. Here indeed is life advancing. There can be no static spirituality for those who follow the progress of truth in this book. It runs the gamut of both Christian teaching and experience. It is centered and circumferenced in Christ.

It includes every possible angle of Christian truth and life, such as—saints in Christ, bonds in Christ, living in Christ, walking in Christ, trusting in Christ, rejoicing in Christ, thinking in Christ, doing in Christ, praying in Christ, citizenship in Christ, steadfastness in Christ, and now farewell in Christ.

The epistle finds us saints in character and leaves us saints in conduct. It finds us in position and leads us to practice. It finds us in life's many Philippis and puts us on life's advancing highway where we "press toward the mark for the prize of the high calling of God in Christ Jesus." Let us now be sure that our life is advancing.

"The grace of our Lord Jesus Christ be with you all. Amen."

PHILIPPIANS

Where Life Advances